CROCHET the CLASSICS

I f you're "hooked" on the whimsical world of Mary Engelbreit, then you'll absolutely adore these cute crocheted creations. Based on her delightfully distinctive artwork, four glorious sections introduce you to the magic of "Mary" décor. *Kitchen Comforts* includes plenty of novel notions — from cheerful checkered placemats to a lovely little teapot warmer. Bright, whimsical flowers and a sunny throw add loads of character to a *Cozy Den*. Enchanting *Bedroom Whimsies* like a cheery cherry wrap and two coordinating pillows look simply splendid in a guest room. And just for fun, crochet some *Fluff 'n' Stuff*: a Scottie dog toy, a fanciful purse, or an exquisite pincushion shaped like a teapot. Choose from these and other "Breit" ideas — 31 in all! Beautiful color photos, clear charts and instructions, and an easy to match color palette (page 5) will inspire you to create a houseful of these appealing accents. So turn the page and get ready to start working on your very own crocheted classic.

THERE'S NO PLACE LIKE HOME

1

Mary Engelbreit

Growing up in St. Louis, Missouri, Mary Engelbreit adored drawing. She began sketching as soon as she could hold a crayon, teaching herself first by copying the work of classic children's illustrators like Jessie Wilcox Smith and Johnny Gruelle, the creator of Raggedy Ann and Raggedy Andy. At age 8, Mary started drawing original artwork, often to accompany a story or book that she was reading. Before long, she had her first "studio" — a hastily vacated linen closet.

"We jammed a desk and chair in there, and I'm sure it was 110 degrees," Mary laughs. "But I would happily sit in that closet for hours at a time and draw pictures."

Her passion for drawing continued to grow, and by the age of 11, Mary knew without a doubt that she wanted to grow up to be an artist. She got her start during high school, selling hand-drawn greeting cards at a local store for 25 cents, then 50 cents. But the nuns

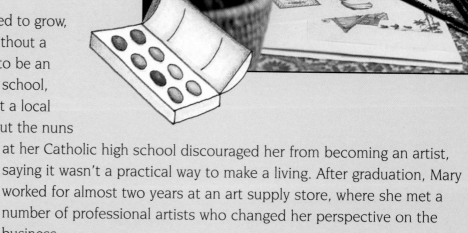

Photo by Rich Saal

at her Catholic high school discouraged her from becoming an artist, saying it wasn't a practical way to make a living. After graduation, Mary worked for almost two years at an art supply store, where she met a number of professional artists who changed her perspective on the business.

"It was a big wake-up call," Mary remembers. "I realized I could live my dream."

After short-lived careers at an ad agency and the St. Louis Post-Dispatch, Mary began working as a free-lance illustrator. In 1977 she married Phil Delano, a social worker, and with his support, Mary started illustrating fantasy greeting cards, depicting dragons, unicorns, castles, and the like. But Mary's style underwent a significant change when her first son was born in 1980.

"Fantasy went out the window, and I began to illustrate reality — there was so much inspiration around me," Mary says. "Suddenly everyday life seemed more interesting to me. I figured that since we probably lived the same kind of life that everyone else seemed to be living, these things must be interesting to them, too."

At this time, Mary began honing her own distinctive style, a richly detailed, nostalgic mixture of whimsical and profound quotes, precocious children like her alter-ego, Ann Estelle, and, of course, her trademark cherries and Scottie dogs.

As Mary found her niche, she decided the time was ripe to start her own greeting card company. She took 12 designs to the National Stationery Show in New York and was thrilled to discover that her work was a hit. A big hit, in fact: by 1986, just three years after her first showing, Mary's greeting card company was making a million dollars a year.

With the incredible reception her art was receiving, Mary took a cue from a fan and chose to license her greeting cards and expand the arena in which her artwork was available. "I always like to share the story of a fan who once told me she wished she could live in my greeting cards. Many fans have written similar letters — that they want to make their homes look like my drawings," Mary confesses.

Now an internationally known artist, Mary has created more than 4,000 images that are featured in her award-winning magazine and on a variety of merchandise, including an exclusive line of craft projects from industry leader Leisure Arts.

But according to Mary, although success is sweet, the ability to spend her days drawing is far better.

"I know it's ridiculous, but I think, 'What do people do if they don't draw?' " she admits. "I have always believed if you choose a job you love, you'll never *work* a day in your life … and to be able to make a living from drawing — I just can't describe what it's like. It's the most satisfying thing I can possibly think of doing. I'm just so fortunate."

Table of Contents

EDITORIAL STAFF
Vice President and Editor-in-Chief:
Sandra Graham Case
Executive Director of Publications:
Cheryl Nodine Gunnells
Senior Director of Publications:
Susan White Sullivan
Director of Designer Relations:
Debra Nettles
Licensed Product Coordinator:
Lisa Truxton Curton
Design Director: Cyndi Hansen
Editorial Director: Susan Frantz Wiles
**Director of Photography, Public Relations,
& Retail Marketing:** Stephen Wilson
Senior Director of Art Operations: Jeff Curtis

TECHNICAL
Leaflet Publications Director: Mary Hutcheson
Managing Editor: Valesha M. Kirksey
Senior Technical Editor: Lois J. Long
Instructional Editor: Sarah J. Green

EDITORIAL
Associate Editor: Kimberly L. Ross

ART
Art Publications Director: Rhonda Shelby
Art Imaging Director: Mark Hawkins
Art Category Manager: Diana Sanders
Lead Graphic Artist: Rebecca J. Hester
Imaging Technicians: Stephanie Johnson and
Mark Potter
Staff Photographer: Russ Ganser
Photography Stylists: Sondra Daniel
Publishing Systems Administrator:
Becky Riddle
Publishing Systems Assistants: Clint Hanson,
Myra Means, and Chris Wertenberger

BUSINESS STAFF
Publisher: Rick Barton
Vice President, Finance: Tom Siebenmorgen
**Director of Corporate Planning and
Development:** Laticia Mull Dittrich
Vice President, Retail Marketing:
Bob Humphrey
Vice President, Sales: Ray Shelgosh
Vice President, National Accounts:
Pam Stebbins
Director of Sales and Services:
Margaret Reinold
Vice President, Operations: Jim Dittrich
Comptroller, Operations: Rob Thieme
Retail Customer Service Managers:
Sharon Hall and Stan Raynor
Print Production Manager: Fred F. Pruss

CREDITS
A special thanks goes to Husqvarna Viking Sewing
Machine Company of Cleveland, Ohio, for providing the
sewing machines used to create several of our projects.

We want to extend a warm *thank you* to Pam Villines for
allowing us to photograph our projects at her home.

To photographers Jerry R. Davis of Jerry Davis
Photography and Ken West of Peerless Photography,
both of Little Rock, Arkansas, we say thank you for your
time, patience, and excellent work.

International Standard Book Number 1-57486-316-9
10 9 8 7 6 5 4 3 2 1

Color Palette

Kitchen Comforts

Wonderfully original crocheted accents are sure to make your kitchen look oh-so smart. Keep your floors tasteful and tidy with sassy checkered rugs in black, white, and scarlet. Coordinating placemats and napkin rings are embellished with your favorite "Mary" motif: cherries, flowers, or Scottie dogs. These cherished themes and more can also be displayed as tiny refrigerator magnets or dainty edgings in thread. And what kitchen would be complete without heartwarming hot pads and a traditional tea cozy? How utterly adorable!

6

PLACEMAT

Shown on pages 7 and 13.

Finished Size: 14" x 18" (35.5 cm x 45.5 cm)

MATERIALS

100% Cotton Worsted Weight Yarn:

Placemat (for one)
Red - 130 yards (119 meters)
White - 55 yards (50.5 meters)
Black - 55 yards (50.5 meters)

Flower (for one)
Red - 10 yards (9 meters)
Green - 10 yards (9 meters)
Yellow - 5 yards (4.5 meters)

Scottie Dog (for one)
Black - 15 yards (13.5 meters)

Cherries (for one)
Red - 5 yards (4.5 meters)
Green - 5 yards (4.5 meters)
Brown - 1 yard (1 meter)

Crochet hook, size H (5 mm) **or** size needed for gauge
Yarn needle
$1/8$" (3 mm) wide Ribbon - 12" (30.5 cm) (for Scottie Dog Only)

GAUGE: 9 dc = $2^1/2$" (6.25 cm);
5 rows = 3" (7.5 cm)

Gauge Swatch: $2^1/2$"w x 3"h
(6.25 cm x 7.5 cm)
With Red, ch 11.
Row 1: Dc in fourth ch from hook **(3 skipped chs count as first dc)** and in each ch across: 9 dc.
Rows 2-5: Ch 3 **(counts as first dc)**, turn; dc in next dc and in each dc across. Finish off.

STITCH GUIDE

TREBLE CROCHET
(abbreviated tr)
YO twice, insert hook in st indicated, YO and pull up a loop (4 loops on hook), (YO and draw through 2 loops on hook) 3 times.

BEGINNING DECREASE
Pull up a loop in first 2 sts, YO and draw through all 3 loops on hook **(counts as one sc)**.

DECREASE
Pull up a loop in next 2 sts, YO and draw through all 3 loops on hook **(counts as one sc)**.

ENDING DECREASE
Pull up a loop in last 2 sc, YO and draw through all 3 loops on hook **(counts as one sc)**.

PLACEMAT
BODY

With Black, ch 65.

Row 1 (Right side): Dc in fourth ch from hook **(3 skipped chs count as first dc)** and in next ch changing to White in last dc made (**Fig. 5, page 94**), ★ dc in next 3 chs changing to Black in last dc made, dc in next 3 chs changing to White in last dc made; repeat from ★ across: 63 dc.

Note: Loop a short piece of yarn around any dc to mark Row 1 as **right** side.

Continue to change colors in same manner.

Row 2: Ch 3 **(counts as first dc, now and throughout)**, turn; dc in next 2 dc, ★ with Black dc in next 3 dc, with White dc in next 3 dc; repeat from ★ across.

Row 3: Ch 3, turn; dc in next 2 dc, ★ with White dc in next 3 dc, with Black dc in next 3 dc; repeat from ★ across.

Row 4: Ch 3, turn; dc in next 2 dc, with Black dc in next 3 dc, with White dc in next 3 dc, do **not** work over Black and White, with Red dc in next 45 dc, with second White dc in next 3 dc, with second Black dc in next 3 dc, with White dc in last 3 dc.

Row 5: Ch 3, turn; dc in next 2 dc, with White dc in next 3 dc, with Black dc in next 3 dc, with Red dc in next 45 dc, with Black dc in next 3 dc, with White dc in next 3 dc, with Black dc in last 3 dc.

Rows 6-20: Repeat Rows 4 and 5, 7 times; then repeat Row 4 once **more**; at end of Row 20, cut first Black, first White, and Red.

Row 21: Ch 3, turn; dc in next 2 dc, ★ with White dc in next 3 dc, with Black dc in next 3 dc; repeat from ★ across.

Row 22: Ch 3, turn; dc in next 2 dc, ★ with Black dc in next 3 dc, with White dc in next 3 dc; repeat from ★ across.

Row 23: Ch 3, turn; dc in next 2 dc, ★ with White dc in next 3 dc, with Black dc in next 3 dc; repeat from ★ across; finish off both colors.

EDGING

Rnd 1: With **right** side facing, join Red with sc in any dc **(see Joining With Sc, page 92)**; sc evenly around working 3 sc in each corner; join with slip st to first sc.

Rnd 2: Ch 1, working from **left** to **right**, work reverse sc in each sc around **(Figs. 9a-d, page 94)**; join with slip st to first st, finish off.

FLOWER
CENTER

Rnd 1 (Right side)**:** With Yellow, ch 2, 6 sc in second ch from hook; join with slip st to first sc.

Note: Mark Rnd 1 as **right** side.

Rnd 2: Ch 1, 2 sc in same st and in each sc around; join with slip st to first sc: 12 sc.

Rnd 3: Slip st in next sc and in each sc around; join with slip st to joining slip st, finish off.

BODY

Rnd 1: With **right** side facing and working **behind** slip sts on Rnd 3 and in sc on Rnd 2, join Red with tr in any sc **(see Joining With Tr, page 93)**; 2 tr in same st and in next sc, (3 tr in next sc, 2 tr in next sc) around; join with slip st to first tr: 30 tr.

Rnd 2: Slip st in next tr and in each tr around; join with slip st to joining slip st, finish off.

FIRST LEAF

Row 1: With **right** side facing and working **behind** slip sts on Rnd 2 of Body and in tr on Rnd 1, join Green with sc in any tr; sc in next 3 tr, leave remaining 26 tr unworked: 4 sc.

Row 2: Ch 1, turn; 2 sc in first sc, sc in next 2 sc, 2 sc in last sc: 6 sc.

Rows 3 and 4: Ch 1, turn; sc in each sc across.

Row 5: Turn; skip first sc, sc in next sc, dc in next 2 sc, sc in next sc, slip st in next sc; finish off.

Continued on page 10.

SECOND LEAF

Row 1: With **right** side facing, join Green with sc in next tr from First Leaf; sc in next 3 tr, leave remaining 22 tr unworked: 4 sc.

Rows 2-5: Work same as First Leaf.

THIRD LEAF

Row 1: With **right** side facing, skip next 8 tr from Second Leaf and join Green with sc in next tr; sc in next 3 tr, leave remaining 10 tr unworked: 4 sc.

Rows 2-5: Work same as First Leaf.

Using photo as a guide for placement, sew Flower to Placemat.

SCOTTIE DOG
FIRST LEG

Ch 5.

Row 1 (Right side)**:** Sc in second ch from hook and in each ch across: 4 sc.

Note: Loop a short piece of yarn around any sc to mark Row 1 as **right** side.

Row 2: Turn; slip st in first sc, sc in last 3 sc; finish off: 3 sc.

SECOND LEG

Work same as First Leg; do **not** finish off.

BODY

Row 1: Turn; sc in first 3 sc, add on 3 sc **(Fig. 6, *page* 94)**, with **right** side of First Leg facing, sc in first sc, work ending decrease: 8 sc.

Rows 2 and 3: Ch 1, turn; sc in each sc across.

Finish off.

MUZZLE

Ch 3.

Row 1: 2 Sc in second ch from hook, sc in last ch; ch 1, with **wrong** side of Body facing, 2 sc in first sc, sc in each sc across: 12 sc and one ch.

Row 2: Ch 2, turn; sc in second ch from hook and in each sc and ch across: 14 sc.

Row 3: Ch 1, turn; sc in each sc across; do **not** finish off.

TAIL

Row 1: Ch 1, turn; sc in first sc, decrease, leave remaining 11 sc unworked: 2 sc.

Row 2: Ch 1, turn; work beginning decrease: one sc.

Row 3: Ch 1, turn; sc in sc; finish off.

HEAD

Row 1: With **right** side of Body facing, skip next 2 sc from Tail and join yarn with slip st in next sc; slip st in next sc, decrease, sc in last 5 sc: 6 sc.

Row 2: Ch 1, turn; work beginning decrease, sc in next 4 sc, leave remaining 2 slip sts unworked: 5 sc.

Row 3: Ch 1, turn; sc in first 3 sc, work ending decrease: 4 sc.

Row 4: Ch 1, turn; work beginning decrease, sc in last 2 sc; do **not** finish off: 3 sc.

FIRST EAR

Row 1: Ch 1, turn; sc in first sc, slip st in next sc, leave remaining sc unworked: 2 sts.

Row 2: Turn; slip st in first slip st, sc in last sc.

Row 3: Ch 1, turn; work beginning decrease; finish off.

SECOND EAR

Row 1: With **right** side facing, join yarn with sc in same st on Row 4 as last slip st of First Ear; slip st in last sc: 2 sts.

Rows 2 and 3: Work same as First Ear.

Using photo as a guide for placement, sew Scottie Dog to Placemat, then tie ribbon around neck.

CHERRIES

CHERRY (Make 2)

Rnd 1 (Right side)**:** With Red, ch 3, 9 hdc in third ch from hook; join with slip st to top of beginning ch-3, finish off: 10 sts.

STEM

With **right** side of one Cherry facing, join Brown with slip st in same st as joining; ch 14, with **right** side of last Cherry facing, slip st in same st as joining; finish off.

FIRST LEAF

Row 1: With **right** side of first Cherry facing, skip first 6 chs on Stem and join Green with sc in next ch (**see Joining With Sc, page 92**); sc in next ch, leave remaining 6 chs unworked: 2 sc.

Row 2: Ch 1, turn; 2 sc in first sc and in last sc: 4 sc.

Row 3: Ch 1, turn; sc in each sc across.

Row 4: Ch 1, turn; work beginning decrease, work ending decrease: 2 sc.

Row 5: Ch 1, turn; work beginning decrease; finish off.

SECOND LEAF

Row 1: With **right** side of First Leaf facing, join Green with sc in same st as last sc on Row 1 of First Leaf; sc in next ch, leave remaining 5 chs unworked: 2 sc.

Rows 2-5: Work same as First Leaf.

Using photo as a guide for placement, sew Cherries to Placemat.

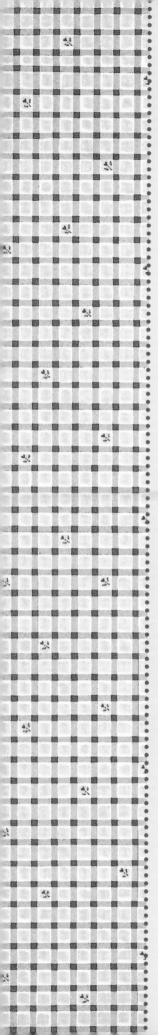

NAPKIN RING

Shown on pages 6 and 13.

Finished Size: 2¼" (5.75 cm) wide

MATERIALS

100% Cotton Worsted Weight Yarn:

Napkin Ring (for one)
- Red ~ 10 yards (9 meters)
- White ~ 5 yards (4.5 meters)
- Black ~ 5 yards (4.5 meters)

Flower
- Red ~ 5 yards (4.5 meters)
- Green ~ 5 yards (4.5 meters)
- Yellow ~ 2 yards (2 meters)

Cherries
- Red ~ 5 yards (4.5 meters)
- Green ~ 5 yards (4.5 meters)
- Brown ~ 1 yard (1 meter)

Scottie Dog Only

100% Cotton Sport Weight Yarn:
- Black ~ 10 yards (9 meters)

Crochet hooks, sizes G (4 mm) **and**
H (5 mm) **or** sizes needed for gauge
Yarn needle
⅛" (3 mm) wide Ribbon ~ 12" (30.5 cm)
(for Scottie Dog Only)

GAUGE: With larger size hook and
worsted weight yarn,
9 dc = 2½" (6.25 cm);
5 rows = 3" (7.5 cm)

Gauge Swatch: 1½"w x 3"h
(3.75 cm x 7.5 cm)
Work same as Napkin Ring for 5 rows.

Use smaller size hook for Scottie Dog
Only.

NAPKIN RING
BODY

With Black, ch 8.

Row 1 (Right side): Dc in fourth ch from hook **(3 skipped chs count as first dc)** and in next ch changing to White in last dc made **(Fig. 5, page 94)**, dc in last 3 chs changing to Black in last dc made: 6 dc.

Note: Loop a short piece of yarn around any dc to mark Row 1 as **right** side.

Continue to change colors in same manner.

Row 2: Ch 3 **(counts as first dc, now and throughout)**, turn; dc in next 2 dc, with White dc in last 3 dc.

Rows 3-8: Ch 3, turn; dc in next 2 dc, with White dc in last 3 dc; at end of Row 8, do **not** change colors, cut Black.

Joining Rnd: Ch 1, turn; with **right** side together and working in free loops of beginning ch **(Fig. 3b, page 93)** and in dc on Rnd 8, slip st in each st across; finish off.

EDGING

Rnd 1: With **right** side facing and working in end of rows on either side, join Red with sc in any row **(see Joining With Sc, page 92)**; sc evenly around; join with slip st to first sc.

Rnd 2: Ch 1, working from **left** to **right**, work reverse sc in same st and in each sc around **(Figs. 9a-d, page 94)**; join with slip st to first st, finish off.

Repeat for opposite side.

Continued on page 14.

13

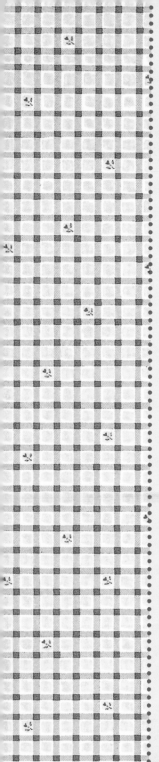

FLOWER
CENTER
Rnd 1 (Right side)**:** With Yellow, ch 2, 6 sc in second ch from hook; join with slip st to first sc.

Note: Mark Rnd 1 as **right** side.

Rnd 2: Slip st in next sc and in each sc around; join with slip st to joining slip st; finish off.

BODY
Rnd 1: With **right** side facing and working **behind** slip sts on Rnd 2 and in sc on Rnd 1, join Red with dc in any sc **(see Joining With Dc, page 93)**; 2 dc in same st and in next sc, (3 dc in next sc, 2 dc in next sc) twice; join with slip st to first dc: 15 dc.

Rnd 2: Slip st in next dc and in each dc around; join with slip st to joining slip st, finish off.

FIRST LEAF
Row 1: With **right** side facing and working **behind** slip sts on Rnd 2 of Body and in dc on Rnd 1, join Green with sc in any dc; sc in next dc, leave remaining 13 dc unworked: 2 sc.

Row 2: Ch 1, turn; 2 sc in first sc and in last sc: 4 sc.

Row 3: Ch 1, turn; skip first sc, dc in next 2 sc, slip st in last sc; finish off.

SECOND LEAF
Row 1: With **right** side facing and working **behind** slip sts on Rnd 2 of Body and in dc on Rnd 1, join Green with sc in next dc from First Leaf; sc in next dc, leave remaining 11 dc unworked: 2 sc.

Rows 2 and 3: Work same as First Leaf.

THIRD LEAF
Row 1: With **right** side facing and working **behind** slip sts on Rnd 2 of Body and in dc on Rnd 1, skip next 5 dc from Second Leaf and join Green with sc in next dc; sc in next dc, leave remaining 4 dc unworked: 2 sc.

Rows 2 and 3: Work same as First Leaf.

Using photo as a guide for placement, sew Flower to Napkin Ring.

SCOTTIE DOG
Using Sport Weight Yarn and smaller size hook, work same as Scottie Dog, page 10.

Using photo as a guide for placement, sew Scottie Dog to Napkin Ring, then tie ribbon around neck.

CHERRIES
Work same as Cherries, page 11.

Using photo as a guide for placement, sew Cherries to Napkin Ring.

TEA POT COZY

Shown on page 7.

Finished Size: 8¹/₂"w x 8"h
(21.5 cm x 20.5 cm)

MATERIALS

100% Cotton Worsted Weight Yarn:

Tea Pot Cozy
Red - 115 yards (105 meters)
White - 35 yards (32 meters)
Black - 35 yards (32 meters)

Flower
Red - 10 yards (9 meters)
Green - 10 yards (9 meters)
Yellow - 5 yards (4.5 meters)

Scottie Dog
Black - 15 yards (13.5 meters)

Cherries
Red - 5 yards (4.5 meters)
Green - 5 yards (4.5 meters)
Brown - 1 yard (1 meter)

Crochet hook, size H (5 mm) **or** size needed for gauge
Yarn needle

GAUGE: 9 dc = 2¹/₂" (6.25 cm);
5 rows = 3" (7.5 cm)

Gauge Swatch: 2¹/₂"w x 3"h
(6.25 cm x 7.5 cm)

With Red, ch 11.
Row 1: Dc in fourth ch from hook and in each ch across **(3 skipped chs count as first dc)**: 9 dc.
Rows 2-5: Ch 3 **(counts as first dc)**, turn; dc in next dc and in each dc across. Finish off.

STITCH GUIDE

TREBLE CROCHET
(*abbreviated tr*)
YO twice, insert hook in st indicated, YO and pull up a loop (4 loops on hook), (YO and draw through 2 loops on hook) 3 times.

DOUBLE TREBLE CROCHET
(*abbreviated dtr*)
YO 3 times, insert hook in st indicated, YO and pull up a loop (5 loops on hook), (YO and draw through 2 loops on hook) 4 times.

2-DC DECREASE (uses next 2 dc)
★ YO, insert hook in **next** dc, YO and pull up a loop, YO and draw through 2 loops on hook; repeat from ★ once **more**, YO and draw through all 3 loops on hook **(counts as one dc)**.

3-DC DECREASE (uses next 3 dc)
★ YO, insert hook in **next** dc, YO and pull up a loop, YO and draw through 2 loops on hook; repeat from ★ 2 times **more**, YO and draw through all 4 loops on hook **(counts as one dc)**.

Continued on page 16.

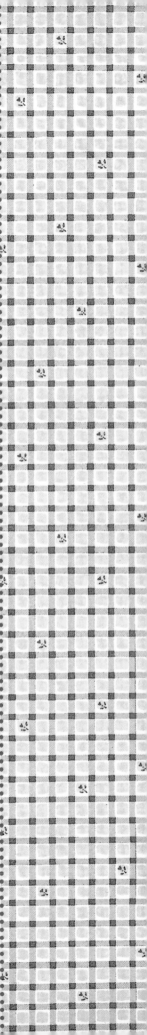

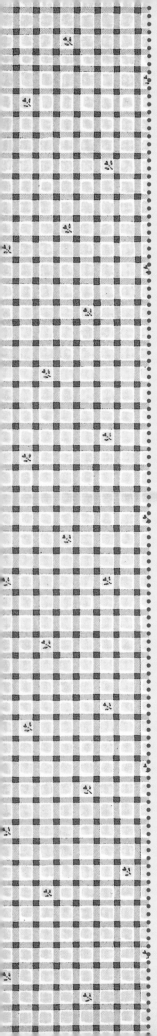

TEA POT COZY
SIDE PIECE (Make 2)
With Black, ch 29.

Row 1: Dc in fourth ch from hook **(3 skipped chs count as first dc, now and throughout)** and in next ch changing to White in last dc made **(Fig. 5, page 94)**, ★ dc in next 3 chs changing to Black in last dc made, dc in next 3 chs changing to White in last dc made; repeat from ★ across: 27 dc.

Continue to change colors in same manner throughout.

Row 2 (Right side)**:** Ch 3 **(counts as first dc, now and throughout)**, turn; dc in next 2 dc, ★ with Black dc in next 3 dc, with White dc in next 3 dc; repeat from ★ across.

Note: Loop a short piece of yarn around any dc to mark Row 2 as **right** side.

Row 3: Ch 3, turn; dc in next 2 dc, ★ with White dc in next 3 dc, with Black dc in next 3 dc; repeat from ★ across.

Row 4: Ch 3, turn; dc in next 2 dc, ★ with Black dc in next 3 dc, with White dc in next 3 dc; repeat from ★ across.

Row 5: Ch 3, turn; dc in next 2 dc, ★ with White dc in next 3 dc, with Black dc in next 3 dc; repeat from ★ across changing to Red in last dc made; cut White and Black.

Rows 6-9: Ch 3, turn; dc in next dc and in each dc across.

Rows 10 and 11: Ch 2, turn; work 2-dc decrease, dc in next dc and in each dc across to last 3 dc, work 3-dc decrease: 19 dc.

Row 12: Ch 1, turn; sc in first dc, hdc in next 2 dc, dc in next 2 dc, tr in next dc, 2 tr in next dc, tr in next dc, dtr in next dc, 3 dtr in next dc, dtr in next dc, tr in next dc, 2 tr in next dc, tr in next dc, dc in next 2 dc, hdc in next 2 dc, sc in last dc; finish off: 23 sts.

END PIECE (Make 2)
With Black, ch 14.

Row 1 (Wrong side)**:** Dc in fourth ch from hook and in next ch, with White dc in next 3 chs, with Black dc in next 3 chs, with White dc in last 3 chs; do **not** finish off: 12 dc.

Note: Mark **back** of any stitch on Row 1 as **right** side.

FIRST HALF
Row 1: Ch 3, turn; dc in next 2 dc, with White dc in next 3 dc, leave remaining 6 dc unworked: 6 dc.

Rows 2 and 3: Ch 3, turn; dc in next 2 dc, with White dc in last 3 dc.

Row 4: Ch 3, turn; dc in next 2 dc, with White dc in last 3 dc changing to Red in last dc made; cut Black and White.

Rows 5-10: Ch 3, turn; dc in next dc and in each dc across.

Finish off.

SECOND HALF
Row 1: With **right** side facing, join Black with dc in next dc from First Half **(see Joining With Dc, page 93)**; dc in next 2 dc, with White dc in last 3 dc: 6 dc.

Rows 2-10: Work same as First Half.

TOP

Row 1: With **right** side of First Half facing, join Red with slip st in first dc; ch 2, dc in next 5 dc; with **right** side of Second Half facing, dc in first 4 dc, work 2-dc decrease: 10 dc.

Rows 2-4: Ch 2, turn; dc in next dc and in each dc across to last 2 dc, work 2-dc decrease: 4 dc.

Row 5: Ch 2, turn; dc in next dc, work 2-dc decrease: 2 dc.

Row 6: Ch 2, turn; dc in next dc; finish off.

JOINING

Row 1: With **wrong** sides of one Side Piece and one End Piece together, matching rows, Side Piece facing, and working in ends of rows, join Red with sc in end of first row **(see Joining With Sc, page 92)**; sc evenly across to center dtr on last row of Side Piece, holding next Side Piece and same End Piece with **wrong** sides together, sc evenly across.

Row 2: Ch 1, working from **left** to **right**, work reverse sc in each sc across **(Figs. 9a-d, page 94)**; finish off.

Repeat for opposite end.

BOTTOM EDGING

Rnd 1: With **right** side facing and working in free loops of beginning chs **(Fig. 3b, page 93)**, join Red with sc in any ch; sc in each ch around; join with slip st to first sc.

Rnd 2: Ch 1, working from **left** to **right**, work reverse sc in same st and in each sc around; join with slip st to first st, finish off.

OPENING EDGING

Rnd 1: With **right** side facing and working in end of rows along opening, join Red with sc in any row; sc evenly around; join with slip st to first sc.

Rnd 2: Ch 1, working from **left** to **right**, work reverse sc in same st and in each sc around; join with slip st to first st, finish off.

Repeat for second opening.

RING

With **right** side facing, join Red with sc at top; ch 10, join with slip st to first ch to form a ring; 15 sc in ring; join with slip st to first sc, finish off.

FLOWER

Work same as Flower, page 9.

Using photo as a guide for placement, sew Flower to Tea Pot Cozy.

SCOTTIE DOG

Work same as Scottie Dog, page 10.

Using photo as a guide for placement, sew Scottie Dog to Tea Pot Cozy.

CHERRIES

Work same as Cherries, page 11.

Using photo as a guide for placement, sew Cherries to Tea Pot Cozy.

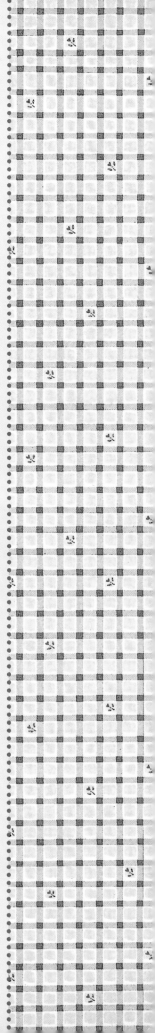

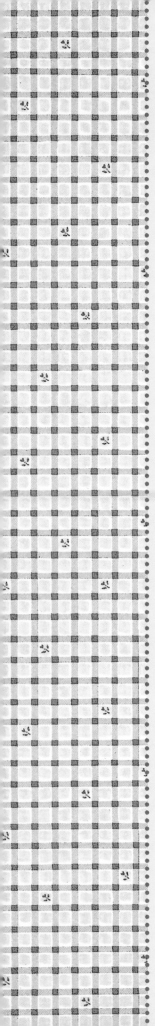

HOT PADS

Shown on page 19.

MATERIALS

100% Cotton Worsted Weight Yarn:

Hot Pad #1
Red - 110 yards (100.5 meters)
Green - 45 yards (41 meters)
Yellow - 25 yards (23 meters)

Hot Pad #2
Red - 125 yards (114.5 meters)
Green - 60 yards (55 meters)
Yellow - 30 yards (27.5 meters)

Hot Pad #3
Red - 140 yards (128 meters)
Green - 45 yards (41 meters)
Yellow - 50 yards (45.5 meters)

Crochet hook, size H (5 mm)
Safety pins
Yarn needle

Note: No gauge is given; your Hot Pads can be a little smaller or a little larger without changing the overall effect.

STITCH GUIDE

BEGINNING DECREASE
Pull up a loop in same st and in next sc, YO and draw through all 3 loops on hook **(counts as one sc)**.

DECREASE
Pull up a loop in next 2 sts, YO and draw through all 3 loops on hook **(counts as one sc)**.

ENDING DECREASE
Pull up a loop in last 2 sc, YO and draw through all 3 loops on hook **(counts as one sc)**.

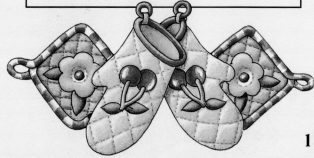

HOT PAD #1
CENTER
BACK

Rnd 1 (Right side): With Yellow, ch 2, 6 sc in second ch from hook; join with slip st to first sc.

Note: Loop a short piece of yarn around any sc to mark Rnd 1 as **right** side.

Rnd 2: Ch 1, 2 sc in same st and in each sc around; join with slip st to first sc: 12 sc.

Rnd 3: Ch 1, sc in same st, 2 sc in next sc, (sc in next sc, 2 sc in next sc) around; join with slip st to first sc: 18 sc.

Rnd 4: Ch 1, 2 sc in same st, sc in next 2 sc, (2 sc in next sc, sc in next 2 sc) around; join with slip st to first sc: 24 sc.

Rnd 5: Ch 1, sc in same st and in next 2 sc, 2 sc in next sc, (sc in next 3 sc, 2 sc in next sc) around; join with slip st to first sc: 30 sc.

Rnd 6: Ch 1, 2 sc in same st, sc in next 4 sc, (2 sc in next sc, sc in next 4 sc) around; join with slip st to first sc, finish off: 36 sc.

FRONT
Work same as Center Back; do **not** finish off: 36 sc.

Joining Rnd: With **wrong** sides of Centers together, Front facing, and working through **both** loops of **both** pieces; ch 1, sc in same st and in next 4 sc, 2 sc in next sc, (sc in next 5 sc, 2 sc in next sc) around; join with slip st to first sc, finish off: 42 sc.

Continued on page 20.

2

1

3

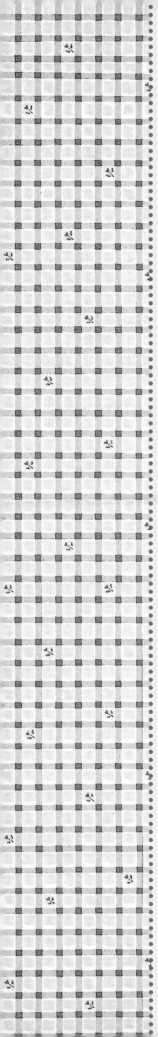

BODY
FRONT
Rnd 1: With Center Front facing and working in Front Loops Only of sc on Joining Rnd **(Fig. 3, page 93)**, join Red with dc in same st as joining **(see Joining With Dc, page 93)**; dc in same st, 2 dc in next sc, (dc in next sc, 2 dc in next sc) around; join with slip st to **both** loops of first dc: 64 dc.

Rnd 2: Ch 1, working in both loops, 2 sc in same st, sc in next 7 dc, (2 sc in next dc, sc in next 7 dc) around; join with slip st to first sc: 72 sc.

Rnd 3: Ch 3 **(counts as first dc, now and throughout)**, dc in same st and in next 8 sc, (2 dc in next sc, dc in next 8 sc) around; join with slip st to first dc: 80 dc.

Rnd 4: Ch 1, 2 sc in same st, sc in next 9 dc, (2 sc in next dc, sc in next 9 dc) around; join with slip st to first sc: 88 sc.

Rnd 5: Ch 3, dc in same st and in next 10 sc, (2 dc in next sc, dc in next 10 sc) around; join with slip st to first dc: 96 dc.

Rnd 6: Ch 1, 2 sc in same st and in next 11 dc, (2 sc in next dc, sc in next 11 dc) around; join with slip st to first sc; finish off leaving a long end for sewing: 104 sc.

BACK
Rnd 1: With Center Back facing and working in free loops of sc on Joining Rnd **(Fig. 3a, page 93)**, join Red with dc in same st as joining; dc in same st, 2 dc in next sc, (dc in next sc, 2 dc in next sc) around; join with slip st to first dc: 64 dc.

Rnds 2-6: Work same as Body Front: 104 sc.

LEAF (Make 2)
With Green, ch 14.

Foundation Row: Sc in second ch from hook and in each ch across: 13 sc.

Rnd 1: Ch 1, turn; working in Front Loops Only, sc in each sc across; **turn**; working in free loops of same sc, sc in each sc across; join with slip st to **both** loops of first sc: 26 sc.

Rnds 2-8: Ch 1, do **not** turn; working in both loops, sc in same st and in each sc around; join with slip st to first sc.

Rnd 9: Ch 1, work beginning decrease, sc in next 9 sc, decrease twice, sc in next 9 sc, work ending decrease; join with slip st to first sc: 22 sc.

Rnd 10: Ch 1, sc in same st and in each sc around; join with slip st to first sc.

Rnd 11: Ch 1, work beginning decrease, sc in next 7 sc, decrease twice, sc in next 7 sc, work ending decrease; join with slip st to first sc: 18 sc.

Rnd 12: Ch 1, sc in same st and in next sc, hdc in next sc, dc in next 3 sc, hdc in next sc, sc in next 4 sc, hdc in next sc, dc in next 3 sc, hdc in next sc, sc in last 2 sc; join with slip st to first sc, finish off leaving a long end for sewing.

Thread needle with long end and sew opening closed.

Using photo as a guide for placement, pin Leaves in place between Front and Back of Body, then sew through **all** thicknesses around entire Body.

HOT PAD #2

CENTER (Make 2)

Rnds 1-6: Work same as Hot Pad #1 Center Back, page 18; do **not** finish off: 36 sc.

Rnd 7: Ch 1, sc in same st and in next 2 sc, 2 sc in next sc, (sc in next 5 sc, 2 sc in next sc) around to last 2 sc, sc in last 2 sc; join with slip st to first sc: 42 sc.

Rnd 8: Ch 1, 2 sc in same st, sc in next 6 sc, (2 sc in next sc, sc in next 6 sc) around; join with slip st to first sc, finish off: 48 sc.

BODY

Joining Rnd: With **wrong** sides of Centers together and working through **outside** loops, join Red with sc in same st as joining (see **Joining With Sc, page 92**); sc in next 6 sc, 2 sc in next sc, (sc in next 7 sc, 2 sc in next sc) around; join with slip st to Front Loop Only of first sc (**Fig. 2, page 93**), do **not** finish off: 54 sc.

FRONT

Rnd 1: Ch 3 (**counts as first dc, now and throughout**), working in Front Loops Only, dc in next sc, (2 dc in next sc, dc in next sc) around; join with slip st to **both** loops of first dc: 80 dc.

Rnd 2: Ch 3, working in both loops, dc in next dc and in each dc around; join with slip st to first dc, do **not** finish off.

FIRST PETAL

Row 1: Ch 3, dc in next 9 dc, leave remaining dc unworked: 10 dc.

Row 2: Ch 3, turn; dc in next 9 dc; finish off.

SECOND THRU SEVENTH PETAL

Row 1: With **right** side facing, join Red with dc in next dc from last Petal made (see **Joining With Dc, page 93**); dc in next 9 dc, leave remaining dc unworked: 10 dc.

Row 2: Ch 3, turn; dc in next 9 dc; finish off.

LAST PETAL

Row 1: With **right** side facing, join Red with dc in next dc from last Petal; dc in last 9 dc: 10 dc.

Row 2: Ch 3, turn; dc in next 9 dc; do **not** finish off.

EDGING

Ch 1, turn; ★ 3 sc in first dc, sc in next 8 dc, 3 sc in last dc, 2 sc in end of next 4 rows; repeat from ★ around; join with slip st to first sc, finish off: 176 sc.

BACK

Rnd 1: With Center Back facing and working in free loops of sc on Joining Rnd of Body (**Fig. 3a, page 93**), join Red with dc in sc after joining; dc in next sc, (2 dc in next sc, dc in next sc) around; join with slip st to **both** loops of first dc: 80 dc.

Complete same as Body Front.

LEAF (Make 2)

With Green, ch 14.

Foundation Row: Sc in second ch from hook and in each ch across: 13 sc.

Rnd 1: Ch 1, turn; working in Front Loops Only, sc in each sc across; **turn**; working in free loops of same sc, sc in each sc across; join with slip st to **both** loops of first sc: 26 sc.

Rnds 2-13: Ch 1, do **not** turn; working in both loops, sc in each sc around; join with slip st to first sc.

Continued on page 22.

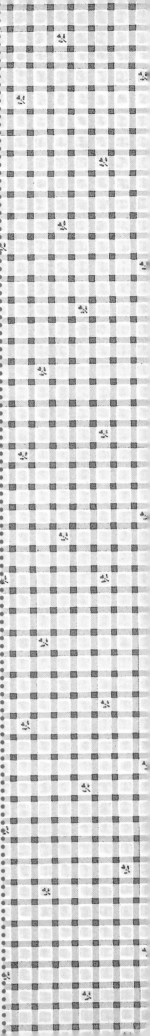

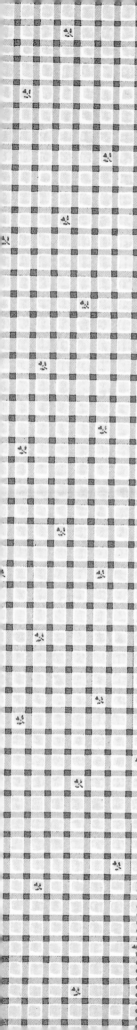

Rnd 14: Ch 1, work beginning decrease, sc in next 9 sc, decrease twice, sc in next 9 sc, work ending decrease; join with slip st to first sc: 22 sc.

Rnd 15: Ch 1, work beginning decrease, sc in next 7 sc, decrease twice, sc in next 7 sc, work ending decrease; join with slip st to first sc: 18 sc.

Rnd 16: Ch 1, work beginning decrease, sc in next 5 sc, decrease twice, sc in next 5 sc, work ending decrease; join with slip st to first sc: 14 sc.

Rnd 17: Ch 1, work beginning decrease, sc in next 3 sc, decrease twice, sc in next 3 sc, work ending decrease; join with slip st to first sc: 10 sc.

Rnd 18: Ch 1, work beginning decrease, sc in next sc, decrease twice, sc in next sc, work ending decrease; join with slip st to first sc: 6 sc.

Rnd 19: Ch 1, work beginning decrease, decrease twice; join with slip st to first sc, finish off leaving a long end for sewing.

Thread needle with long end and weave through sc on Rnd 19; gather tightly and secure end.

Using photo as a guide for placement, pin Leaves in place between Front and Back of Body, then sew through **all** thicknesses around entire Body.

HOT PAD #3
CENTER
BACK
Rnds 1-6: Work same as Hot Pad #1 Center Back, page 18; do **not** finish off: 36 sc.

Rnd 7: Ch 1, sc in same st and in next 4 sc, 2 sc in next sc, (sc in next 5 sc, 2 sc in next sc) around; join with slip st to first sc, finish off: 42 sc.

FRONT
Rnds 1-7: Work same as Center Back; do **not** finish off: 42 sc.

Rnd 8 (Joining Rnd): With **wrong** sides of Center together, Front facing, and working through **both** loops on **both** pieces; ch 1, 2 sc in same st, sc in next 6 sc, (2 sc in next sc, sc in next 6 sc) around; join with slip st to first sc: 48 sc.

Rnd 9: Ch 1, sc in same st and in next 6 sc, 2 sc in next sc, (sc in next 7 sc, 2 sc in next sc) around; join with slip st to first sc: 54 sc.

Rnd 10: Ch 1, sc in same st and in next 7 sc, 2 sc in next sc, (sc in next 8 sc, 2 sc in next sc) around; join with slip st to first sc: 60 sc.

Rnd 11: Ch 1, sc in same st and in next 8 sc, 2 sc in next sc, (sc in next 9 sc, 2 sc in next sc) around; join with slip st to first sc: 66 sc.

Rnd 12: Ch 1, sc in same st and in next 9 sc, 2 sc in next sc, (sc in next 10 sc, 2 sc in next sc) around; join with slip st to first sc: 72 sc.

Rnd 13: Ch 1, sc in same st and in next 10 sc, 2 sc in next sc, (sc in next 11 sc, 2 sc in next sc) around; join with slip st to first sc, finish off: 78 sc.

Rnd 14: With Center Front facing, join Red with sc in same st as joining **(see Joining With Sc, page 92)**; sc in next 5 sc, (2 sc in next sc, sc in next 5 sc) around; join with slip st to Front Loop Only of first sc **(Fig. 2, page 93)**, do **not** finish off: 90 sc.

FRONT PETALS
Rnd 1: Ch 1, sc in Front Loop Only of same st and each sc around; join with slip st to **both** loops of first sc; do **not** finish off.

FIRST PETAL

Row 1: Ch 1, turn; working in both loops, 2 sc in first sc, sc in next 8 sc, 2 sc in next sc, leave remaining 80 sc unworked: 12 sc.

Rows 2-7: Ch 1, turn; 2 sc in first sc, sc in each sc across to last sc, 2 sc in last sc: 24 sc.

Rows 8-10: Ch 1, turn; sc in each sc across.

Finish off.

SECOND PETAL

Row 1: With **wrong** side facing, skip next 20 sc from Petal just made and join Red with sc in next sc; sc in same st, sc in next 8 sc, 2 sc in next sc, leave remaining sc unworked: 12 sc.

Rows 2-10: Work same as First Petal.

Finish off.

THIRD PETAL

Work same as Second Petal; do **not** finish off.

EDGING

Ch 1, turn; ★ 3 sc in first sc, sc in next 22 sc, 3 sc in last sc; sc in end of each row across; sc in next 20 skipped sc on Rnd 1; sc in end of each row across; repeat from ★ 2 times **more**; join with slip st to first sc, finish off.

BACK PETALS

Rnd 1: With Center Back facing and working in free loops of sc on Rnd 14 of Center Front (**Fig. 3a, page 93**), skip first 8 sc from joining and join Red with sc in next sc; sc in each sc around; join with slip st to **both** loops of first sc; do **not** finish off.

Complete same as Front Petals.

LEAF (Make 2)

Work same as Hot Pad #1 Leaf, page 20, through Rnd 7: 26 sc.

Rnds 8-13: Work same as Rnds 14-19 of Hot Pad #2 Leaf, page 22: 3 sc.

Thread needle with long end and weave through sc on Rnd 13; gather tightly and secure end.

FINISHING

Using Diagram as a guide for placement:

Working through **both** thicknesses of Row 1 of Petals and in sc on Edging **between** Petals, sew around entire Center.

Pin one Leaf **between** First Petals along left edge, matching beginning ch of Leaf and Edging on Petals, working through **all** thicknesses, sew edge together.

Repeat on Second Petal with second Leaf.

Sew opposite edge of First and Second Petals and both edges on Third Petal.

Using photo as a guide, fold Petals over Center and tack in place.

DIAGRAM

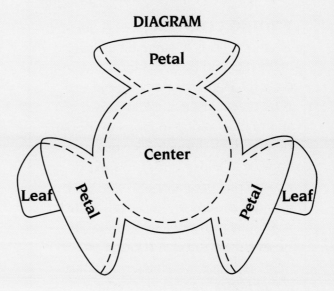

LEAF EDGING

Shown on page 25.

Finished Size: 1³/₄" (4.5 cm) wide

MATERIALS

Bedspread Weight Cotton Thread
  (size 10):
  10 yards (9 meters)
    per 4" (10 cm) length of Edging
Steel crochet hook, size 7 (1.65 mm) **or**
  size needed for gauge

GAUGE SWATCH: 1³/₄"w x 4"l
                    (4.5 cm x 10 cm)
Rows 1-10: Work same as Edging.

STITCH GUIDE

BEGINNING CLUSTER
  (uses first 5 dc)
Ch 2, turn; ★ YO, insert hook in **next** dc, YO and pull up a loop, YO and draw through 2 loops on hook; repeat from ★ 3 times **more**; YO and draw through all 5 loops on hook.

ENDING CLUSTER (uses 6 dc)
YO, insert hook in same dc as last dc made, YO and pull up a loop, YO and draw through 2 loops on hook, YO 3 times, insert hook in next dc, YO and pull up a loop (6 loops on hook), YO and draw through 2 loops on hook, ★ YO, insert hook in **next** dc, YO and pull up a loop, YO and draw through 2 loops on hook; repeat from ★ 3 times **more** (9 loops on hook), YO and draw through 6 loops on hook, (4 loops remaining on hook), YO and draw through 2 loops on hook, YO and draw through all 3 loops on hook.

EDGING

Row 1: Ch 8, dc in eighth ch from hook **(first 7 chs count as first dc plus ch 4)**: 2 dc and one ch-4 sp.

Row 2: Ch 3 **(counts as first dc, now and throughout)**, turn; 4 dc in first dc, ch 3, dc in next ch-4 sp, ch 3, 5 dc in last dc: 11 dc and 2 ch-3 sps.

Row 3: Ch 3, turn; dc in next 4 dc, ch 3, (dc, ch 4, dc) in next dc, ch 3, dc in last 5 dc: 12 dc and 3 sps.

Row 4: Work Beginning Cluster, ch 3, 5 dc in next dc, ch 3, dc in next ch-4 sp, ch 3, 4 dc in next dc, work Ending Cluster.

Repeat Rows 3 and 4 until Edging measures approximately ¹/₄" (7 mm) less than desired length, ending by working Row 3.

Last Row: Work Beginning Cluster, ch 3, slip st in next dc and in next 4 chs, slip st in next dc, ch 3, ★ YO, insert hook in **next** dc, YO and pull up a loop, YO and draw through 2 loops on hook; repeat from ★ 4 times **more**, YO and draw through all 6 loops on hook, finish off.

See Washing and Blocking, page 95.

FLOWER EDGING #1

Shown at lower left on page 25.

Finished Size: 1¼" (3.25 cm) wide

MATERIALS

Bedspread Weight Cotton Thread
(size 10):
Red ~ 5 yards (4.5 meters)
Green ~ 5 yards (4.5 meters)
Yellow ~ 1 yard (1 meter)
Note: Thread amounts are for
one Flower.
Steel crochet hook, size 5 (1.9 mm) **or**
size needed for gauge

GAUGE: Each Flower = 1¼" (3.25 cm)

Gauge Swatch: ¾" (19 mm) diameter
Work same as Center of First Flower.

STITCH GUIDE

BEGINNING DECREASE
Pull up a loop in first 2 sc, YO and
draw through all 3 loops on hook
(counts as one sc).

ENDING DECREASE
Pull up a loop in last 2 sc, YO and
draw through all 3 loops on hook
(counts as one sc).

FIRST FLOWER
CENTER

Rnd 1 (Right side): With Yellow, ch 2, 6 sc
in second ch from hook; join with slip st
to first sc.

Note: Loop a short piece of thread
around any sc to mark Rnd 1 as **right**
side.

Rnd 2: Ch 1, 2 sc in same st and in each
sc around; join with slip st to first sc:
12 sc.

Rnd 3: Ch 1, 2 sc in same st, sc in next
sc, (2 sc in next sc, sc in next sc) around;
join with slip st to first sc, finish off:
18 sc.

BODY

Rnd 1: With **right** side facing, join Red
with hdc in any sc **(see Joining With Hdc,
page 93)**; hdc in same st, 2 hdc in each
of next 4 sc, hdc in next sc, (2 hdc in
each of next 3 sc, hdc in next sc) around;
join with slip st to Front Loop Only of first
hdc **(Fig. 2, page 92)**: 32 hdc.

Rnd 2: Working in Front Loops Only,
(slip st, ch 2, hdc) in next hdc, hdc in next
hdc, place marker in free loop of last hdc
worked into for Leaf placement, hdc in
next hdc, ★ (hdc, ch 2, slip st) in next
hdc, (slip st, ch 2, hdc) in next hdc, hdc in
next 2 hdc; repeat from ★ 6 times **more**,
hdc in same st as joining, ch 2; join with
slip st to joining slip st, finish off:
8 petals.

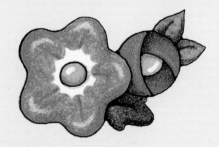

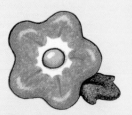

26

FIRST LEAF

Row 1: With **right** side facing, working **behind** petals on Rnd 2 and in free loops of hdc on Rnd 1 **(Fig. 3a, page 93)**, join Green with hdc in marked hdc; hdc in next 3 hdc, leave remaining 28 hdc unworked: 4 hdc.

Row 2: Ch 1, turn; working in both loops, 2 sc in first hdc, sc in next 2 hdc, 2 sc in last hdc: 6 sc.

Row 3: Ch 1, turn; sc in each sc across.

Row 4: Ch 1, turn; work beginning decrease, sc in next 2 sc, work ending decrease: 4 sc.

Row 5: Ch 1, turn; work beginning decrease, work ending decrease: 2 sc.

Row 6: Ch 1, turn; work beginning decrease; finish off.

SECOND LEAF

Row 1: With **right** side facing, working **behind** petals on Rnd 2 and in free loops of hdc on Rnd 1, join Green with hdc in same st as last hdc on Row 1 of First Leaf; hdc in next 3 hdc, leave remaining 25 hdc unworked: 4 hdc.

Rows 2-6: Work same as First Leaf.

THIRD LEAF

Row 1: With **right** side facing, working **behind** petals on Rnd 2 and in free loops of hdc on Rnd 1, skip next 9 hdc from Second Leaf and join Green with hdc in next hdc; hdc in next 3 hdc, leave remaining 12 hdc unworked: 4 hdc.

Rows 2-6: Work same as First Leaf.

FOURTH LEAF

Row 1: With **right** side facing, working **behind** petals on Rnd 2 and in free loops of hdc on Rnd 1, join Green with hdc in same st as last hdc on Row 1 of Third Leaf; hdc in next 3 hdc, leave remaining 9 hdc unworked: 4 hdc.

Rows 2-6: Work same as First Leaf.

SECOND FLOWER

Work same as First Flower through Second Leaf.

THIRD LEAF

Rows 1-5: Work same as First Flower: 2 sc.

Row 6: Ch 1, turn; work beginning decrease, holding **previous** Flower with **wrong** side facing, slip st in sc on **adjacent** Leaf on **previous** Flower; finish off.

FOURTH LEAF

Rows 1-5: Work same as First Flower: 2 sc.

Row 6: Ch 1, turn; work beginning decrease, holding **previous** Flower with **wrong** side facing, slip st in sc on next Leaf on **previous** Flower; finish off.

Repeat Second Flower as many times as desired.

See Washing and Blocking, page 95.

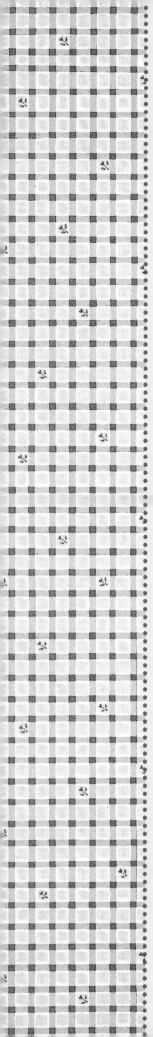

HEART EDGING

Shown on page 25.

Finished Size: 1" (2.5 cm) wide

MATERIALS

Bedspread Weight Cotton Thread
(size 10):
5 yards (4.5 meters)
per 3" (2.5 cm) length of Edging
Steel crochet hook, size 7 (1.65 mm) **or**
size needed for gauge

GAUGE SWATCH: 1"w x 3"l
(2.5 cm x 7.5 cm)
Work First Heart and 5 Second Hearts.

FIRST HEART

Row 1: Ch 4, 4 dc in fourth ch from hook **(3 skipped chs count as first dc, now and throughout)**: 5 dc.

Row 2: Ch 4, turn; dc in fourth ch from hook, skip first 2 dc, slip st in next dc, ch 4, dc in fourth ch from hook, skip next dc, slip st in last dc; do **not** finish off.

SECOND HEART

Row 1: Ch 4, do **not** turn; 4 dc in fourth ch from hook: 5 dc.

Row 2: Ch 4, turn; dc in fourth ch from hook, skip first 2 dc, slip st in next dc, ch 4, dc in fourth ch from hook, skip next dc, slip st in last dc; do **not** finish off.

Repeat Second Heart until Edging is desired length; finish off.

See Washing and Blocking, page 95.

FLOWER EDGING #2

Shown on center hanging towel on page 25.

Finished Size: 1¼" (3.25 cm) wide

MATERIALS

Bedspread Weight Cotton Thread
(size 10):
Red - 5 yards (4.5 meters)
Green - 5 yards (4.5 meters)
Yellow - 1 yard (1 meter)
Note: Thread amounts are for
one Flower.
Steel crochet hook, size 5 (1.9 mm) **or**
size needed for gauge

GAUGE: Each Flower = 1¼" (3.25 cm)

Gauge Swatch: ½" (12 mm) diameter
Work same as Center of First Flower.

STITCH GUIDE

TREBLE CROCHET
(**abbreviated tr**)
YO twice, insert hook in st indicated,
YO and pull up a loop (4 loops on
hook), (YO and draw through 2 loops
on hook) 3 times.

BEGINNING DECREASE
Pull up a loop in first 2 sc, YO and
draw through all 3 loops on hook
(**counts as one sc**).

ENDING DECREASE
Pull up a loop in last 2 sc, YO and
draw through all 3 loops on hook
(**counts as one sc**).

FIRST FLOWER
CENTER
Rnd 1 (Right side)**:** With Yellow, ch 2, 6 sc
in second ch from hook; join with slip st
to first sc.

Note: Loop a short piece of thread
around any sc to mark Rnd 1 as **right**
side.

Rnd 2: Ch 1, 2 sc in same st and in each
sc around; join with slip st to first sc:
12 sc.

Rnd 3: Slip st in next sc and in each sc
around; join with slip st to joining slip st,
finish off.

BODY
Rnd 1: With **right** side facing, working
behind slip sts on Rnd 3 and in sc on
Rnd 2, join Red with tr in any sc (**see
Joining With Tr, page 93**); 2 tr in same st
and in next sc, (3 tr in next sc, 2 tr in next
sc) around; join with slip st to first tr:
30 tr.

Rnd 2: Slip st in next tr and in each tr
around; join with slip st to joining slip st,
finish off.

FIRST SIDE
Foundation Row: With **right** side facing,
working **behind** slip sts on Rnd 2 of Body
and in tr on Rnd 1, join Green with sc in
any tr (**see Joining With Sc, page 92**); sc
in next 6 tr, leave remaining 23 tr
unworked: 7 sc.

Continued on page 30.

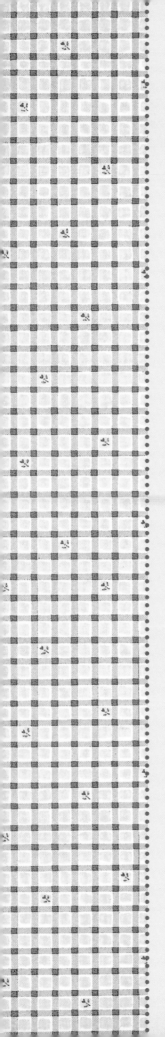

FIRST LEAF

Row 1: Ch 1, turn; 2 sc in first sc, sc in next 2 sc, 2 sc in Back Loop Only of next sc **(Fig. 2, *page* 93)**, leave remaining 3 sc unworked: 6 sc.

Row 2: Ch 1, turn; sc in each sc across.

Row 3: Ch 1, turn; work beginning decrease, sc in next 2 sc, work ending decrease: 4 sc.

Row 4: Ch 1, turn; work beginning decrease, work ending decrease: 2 sc.

Row 5: Ch 1, turn; work beginning decrease; finish off.

SECOND LEAF

Row 1: With **wrong** side facing, join Green with sc in free loop of same sc as last sc on Row 1 of First Leaf **(Fig. 3a, *page* 93)**; sc in same st, working in **both** loops, sc in next 2 sc, 2 sc in last sc: 6 sc.

Rows 2-5: Work same as First Leaf.

SECOND SIDE

Foundation Row: With **right** side facing, working **behind** slip sts on Rnd 2 of Body and in tr on Rnd 1, skip next 8 tr from First Side and join Green with sc in next tr; sc in next 6 tr, leave remaining 8 tr unworked: 7 sc.

Complete same as First Side.

SECOND FLOWER

Work same as First Flower through Foundation Row on Second Side.

FIRST LEAF

Rows 1-4: Work same as First Leaf on First Side of First Flower: 2 sc.

Row 5: Ch 1, turn; work beginning decrease, holding **previous** Flower with **wrong** side facing, slip st in sc on **adjacent** Leaf on **previous** Flower; finish off.

SECOND LEAF

Rows 1-4: Work same as Second Leaf on First Side of First Flower: 2 sc.

Row 5: Ch 1, turn; work beginning decrease, holding **previous** Flower with **wrong** side facing, slip st in sc on next Leaf on **previous** Flower; finish off.

Repeat Second Flower as many times as desired.

See Washing and Blocking, page 95.

BLOCK EDGING

Shown on page 25.

Finished Size: 1¼" (3.25 cm) wide

MATERIALS
Bedspread Weight Cotton Thread
   (size 10):
   5 yards (4.5 meters)
      per 4" (10 cm) length of Edging
Steel crochet hook, size 7 (1.65 mm) **or**
   size needed for gauge

GAUGE SWATCH: 1¼"w x 4"l
                  (3.25 cm x 10 cm)
Work same as Edging for 30 rows.

EDGING
Ch 6.

Row 1 (Right side)**:** Sc in second ch from hook and in each ch across: 5 sc.

Rows 2-5: Ch 1, turn; sc in each sc across.

Row 6: Ch 6, turn; sc in second ch from hook and in each ch across, leave remaining 5 sc unworked.

Rows 7-10: Ch 1, turn; sc in each sc across.

Repeat Rows 6-10 until Edging measures desired length, ending by working Row 10; finish off.

See Washing and Blocking, page 95.

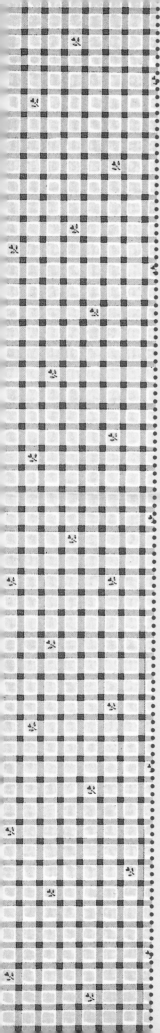

MAGNETS
Shown on page 25.

MATERIALS
Bedspread Weight Cotton Thread (size 10):

Flower #1
Red - 35 yards (32 meters)
Green - 20 yards (18.5 meters)
Yellow - 10 yards (9 meters)

Flower #2
Red - 20 yards (18.5 meters)
Green - 20 yards (18.5 meters)
Yellow - 10 yards (9 meters)

Scottie Dog
Black - 25 yards (23 meters)

Cherries
Red - 15 yards (13.5 meters)
Brown - 5 yards (4.5 meters)
Green - 20 yards (18.5 meters)

Steel crochet hook, size 5 (1.9 mm)
Safety pins
Polyester fiberfill (for Cherries Only)
Tapestry needle
Magnets
Glue

Note: No gauge is given; your Magnets can be a little smaller or larger without changing the overall effect.

STITCH GUIDE

TREBLE CROCHET
(abbreviated tr)
YO twice, insert hook in st indicated, YO and pull up a loop (4 loops on hook), (YO and draw through 2 loops on hook) 3 times.

BEGINNING DECREASE
Pull up a loop in same st and in next sc, YO and draw through all 3 loops on hook **(counts as one sc)**.

DECREASE
Pull up a loop in next 2 sts, YO and draw through all 3 loops on hook **(counts as one sc)**.

ENDING DECREASE
Pull up a loop in last 2 sc, YO and draw through all 3 loops on hook **(counts as one sc)**.

FLOWER #1 *(shown at top left)*
CENTER
BACK
Rnd 1 (Right side)**:** With Yellow, ch 2, 6 sc in second ch from hook; join with slip st to first sc.

Note: Loop a short piece of thread around any sc to mark Rnd 1 as **right** side.

Rnd 2: Ch 1, 2 sc in same st and in each sc around; join with slip st to first sc: 12 sc.

Rnd 3: Ch 1, sc in same st, 2 sc in next sc, (sc in next sc, 2 sc in next sc) around; join with slip st to first sc: 18 sc.

Rnd 4: Ch 1, 2 sc in same st, sc in next 2 sc, (2 sc in next sc, sc in next 2 sc) around; join with slip st to first sc: 24 sc.

Rnd 5: Ch 1, sc in same st and in next 2 sc, 2 sc in next sc, (sc in next 3 sc, 2 sc in next sc) around; join with slip st to Back Loop Only of first sc **(Fig. 2, page 93)**, finish off: 30 sc.

FRONT
Work same as Center Back, do **not** finish off: 30 sc.

Joining Rnd: With **wrong** sides of Centers together, Front facing, and working through **inside** loops only, slip st in each sc around; join with slip st to **both** loops of first slip st, finish off.

BODY
FRONT

Rnd 1: With Center Front facing and working in free loops of sc on Rnd 5 **(Fig. 3a, page 93)**, join Red with dc in same st as joining **(see Joining With Dc, page 93)**; dc in same st, 2 dc in each of next 2 sc, dc in next 2 sc, (2 dc in each of next 3 sc, dc in next 2 sc) around; join with slip st to first dc: 48 dc.

Rnd 2: Ch 1, 2 sc in same st, sc in next 7 dc, (2 sc in next dc, sc in next 7 dc) around; join with slip st to first sc: 54 sc.

Rnd 3: Ch 3 **(counts as first dc, now and throughout)**, dc in next 3 sc, 2 dc in next sc, (dc in next 8 sc, 2 dc in next sc) around to last 4 sc, dc in last 4 sc; join with slip st to first dc: 60 dc.

Rnd 4: Ch 1, 2 sc in same st, sc in next 9 dc, (2 sc in next dc, sc in next 9 dc) around; join with slip st to first sc, finish off: 66 sc.

BACK

With Center Back facing, work same as Body Front: 66 sc.

LEAF (Make 2)
Work same as Hot Pad #1 Leaf, page 20.

Using photo as a guide for placement, pin Leaves in place between Front and Back of Body, then sew through **all** thicknesses around entire Body.

Glue magnet to wrong side.

FLOWER #2 (shown at bottom left)
CENTER (Make 2)
Rnd 1 (Right side): With Yellow, ch 2, 6 sc in second ch from hook; join with slip st to first sc.

Note: Loop a short piece of thread around any sc to mark Rnd 1 as **right** side.

Rnd 2: Ch 1, 2 sc in same st and in each sc around; join with slip st to first sc: 12 sc.

Rnd 3: Ch 1, sc in same st, 2 sc in next sc, (sc in next sc, 2 sc in next sc) around; join with slip st to first sc: 18 sc.

Rnd 4: Ch 1, 2 sc in same st, sc in next 2 sc, (2 sc in next sc, sc in next 2 sc) around; join with slip st to first sc: 24 sc.

Rnd 5: Ch 1, sc in same st and in next 2 sc, 2 sc in next sc, (sc in next 3 sc, 2 sc in next sc) around; join with slip st to first sc: 30 sc.

Rnd 6: Ch 1, 2 sc in same st, sc in next 4 sc, (2 sc in next sc, sc in next 4 sc) around; join with slip st to first sc: 36 sc.

Rnd 7: Ch 1, sc in same st and in next 4 sc, 2 sc in next sc, (sc in next 5 sc, 2 sc in next sc) around; join with slip st to first sc, finish off: 42 sc.

Joining Rnd: With **wrong** sides of Centers together and working through **inside** loops only, join Red with slip st in any sc; slip st in each sc around; join with slip st to first slip st, finish off.

BODY
FRONT
Rnd 1: With Center facing and working in free loops of sc on Rnd 7 **(Fig. 3a, page 93)**, join Red with slip st in any sc; ch 4 **(counts as first tr)**, tr in same st, 2 tr in next sc, (tr in next sc, 2 tr in next sc) around; join with slip st to first tr: 64 tr.

Rnd 2: Slip st in next tr, ch 2, tr in next 6 tr, ch 2, (slip next 2 tr, ch 2, tr in next 6 tr, ch 2) around; join with slip st to joining slip st, finish off.

BACK
Working on opposite side of Center, work same as Body Front.

33

Continued on page 34.

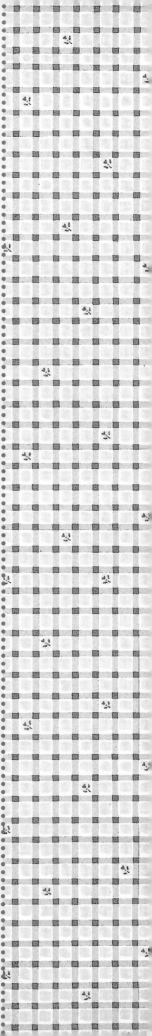

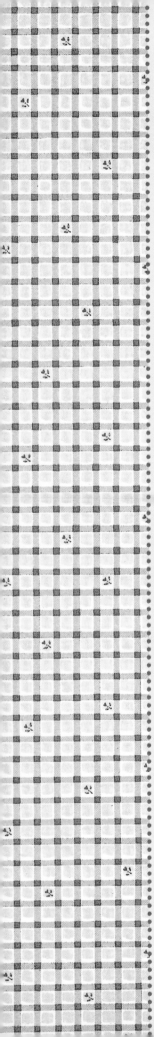

LEAF (Make 2)

With Green, ch 14.

Foundation Row: Sc in second ch from hook and in each ch across: 13 sc.

Rnd 1: Ch 1, turn; working in Front Loops Only (**Fig. 2**, *page 92*), sc in each sc across; **turn**; working in free loops of same sc, sc in each sc across; join with slip st to **both** loops of first sc: 26 sc.

Rnds 2-7: Ch 1, do **not** turn; working in both loops, sc in each sc around; join with slip st to first sc.

Rnds 8-14: Work same as Rnds 14-19 of Hot Pad #2 Leaf, page 22.

Thread needle with long end and weave through sc on Rnd 14; gather tightly and secure end.

Using photo as a guide for placement, pin Leaves in place between Front and Back of Body, then sew through **all** thicknesses.

Glue magnet to wrong side.

SCOTTIE DOG

SIDE (Make 2)

FIRST LEG

Ch 10.

Row 1 (Right side): Sc in second ch from hook and in each across: 9 sc.

Note: Loop a short piece of thread around any sc to mark Row 1 as **right** side.

Row 2: Turn; slip st in first sc, sc in each sc across: 8 sc.

Row 3: Ch 1, turn; sc in first 7 sc, leave remaining sc unworked; finish off.

SECOND LEG

Ch 9.

Row 1 (Right side): Sc in second ch from hook and in each across: 8 sc.

Note: Mark Row 1 as **right** side.

Row 2: Turn; slip st in first sc, sc in each sc across: 7 sc.

Row 3: Ch 1, turn; sc in first 6 sc, leave remaining sc unworked; do **not** finish off.

BODY

Row 1: Turn; slip st in first sc, sc in last 5 sc, add on 7 sc (**Fig. 6**, *page 94*), with **wrong** side of First Leg facing, sc in each sc across: 19 sc.

Row 2: Ch 1, turn; sc in each sc across.

Row 3: Ch 1, turn; sc in each sc across to last 2 sc, work ending decrease: 18 sc.

Row 4: Ch 1, turn; sc in each sc across.

Row 5: Ch 1, turn; 2 sc in first sc, sc in each sc across to last sc, 2 sc in last sc: 20 sc.

Row 6: Ch 1, turn; 2 sc in first sc, sc in each sc across; finish off: 21 sc.

MUZZLE

Ch 4.

Row 1 (Right side): Sc in second ch from hook and in last 2 chs: 3 sc.

Note: Mark Row 1 as **right** side.

Row 2: Ch 1, turn; sc in each sc across, add on 2 sc, with **wrong** side of Body facing, sc in each sc across to last sc, 2 sc in last sc: 27 sc.

Rows 3 and 4: Ch 1, turn; sc in each sc across.

Row 5: Ch 1, turn; sc in first 3 sc, decrease, slip st in next 3 sc, sc in each sc across to last sc, 2 sc in last sc; do **not** finish off: 24 sc.

HEAD

Row 1: Ch 1, turn; sc in first 11 sc, decrease, leave remaining 14 sts unworked: 12 sc.

34

Row 2: Ch 1, turn; sc in each sc across to last 2 sc, work ending decrease: 11 sc.

Row 3: Ch 1, turn; [pull up a loop in first 2 sts, YO and draw through all 3 loops on hook **(beginning decrease made)(counts as one sc)]**, sc in each sc across to last 2 sc, work ending decrease: 9 sc.

Row 4: Ch 1, turn; 2 sc in first sc, sc in each sc across to last 2 sc, work ending decrease.

Row 5: Ch 1, turn; work beginning decrease, sc in each sc across: 8 sc.

Row 6: Ch 1, turn; work beginning decrease, sc in each sc across to last 2 sc, work ending decrease: 6 sc.

Row 7: Ch 1, turn; sc in each sc across to last 2 sc, work ending decrease; do **not** finish off: 5 sc.

FIRST EAR

Row 1: Ch 1, turn; sc in first sc, decrease, leave remaining 2 sc unworked: 2 sc.

Row 2: Ch 1, turn; work beginning decrease: one sc.

Row 3: Ch 1, turn; sc in sc; finish off.

SECOND EAR

Row 1: With **right** side facing, join thread with sc in same st on Row 7 as last sc of First Ear **(see Joining With Sc, page 92)**; work ending decrease: 2 sc.

Row 2: Ch 1, turn; work beginning decrease: one sc.

Row 3: Ch 1, turn; sc in sc; finish off.

JOINING

Holding both pieces together with **right** side of top Side Piece facing, join thread with sc in any sc; sc evenly around entire piece increasing and decreasing as needed to keep piece laying flat; join with slip st to first sc, finish off.

Glue magnets to wrong side.

CHERRIES
CHERRY (Make 2)

Rnd 1 (Right side)**:** With Red, ch 2, 6 sc in second ch from hook; do **not** join, place marker **(see Markers, page 90)**.

Rnd 2: 2 Sc in each sc around: 12 sc.

Rnd 3: 2 Sc in next sc, sc in next sc, (2 sc in next sc, sc in next sc) around: 18 sc.

Rnd 4: 2 Sc in next sc, sc in next 2 sc, (2 sc in next sc, sc in next 2 sc) around: 24 sc.

Rnds 5-9: Sc in each sc around.

Rnd 10: (Decrease, sc in next 2 sc) around: 18 sc.

Stuff Cherry.

Rnd 11: (Decrease, sc in next sc) around: 12 sc.

Rnds 12 and 13: Decrease around: 3 sc.

Finish off.

Continued on page 36.

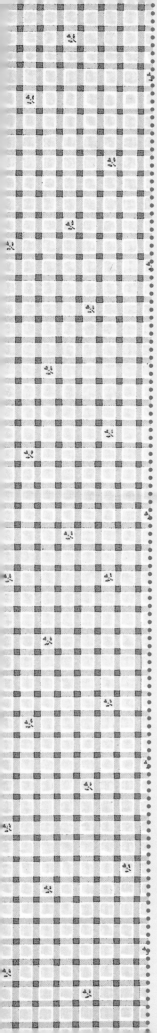

STEM

Join Brown with slip st at top of one Cherry; ch 1, turn; sc in slip st, **turn**; sc in horizontal loop at left side of sc **(Fig. 1a)**, ★ **turn**; sc in horizontal loops at left side of sc **(Fig. 1b)**; repeat from ★ until Stem measures 1³/₄"; finish off.

Fig. 1a

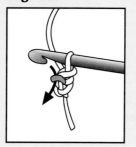

Fig. 1b

Repeat for second Cherry.

LEAF (Make 2)

Foundation Row: With Green, ch 2, sc in second ch from hook: one sc.

Rnd 1 (Right side): Ch 1, turn; 3 sc in Front Loop Only of sc **(Fig. 2, page 92)**, **turn**; 3 sc in free loop of same sc **(Fig. 3a, page 93)**; join with slip st to **both** loops of first sc: 6 sc.

Note: Mark Rnd 1 as **right** side.

Rnd 2: Ch 1, do **not** turn; working in both loops, 2 sc in first sc, sc in next sc, 2 sc in each of next 2 sc, sc in next sc, 2 sc in last sc; join with slip st to first sc: 10 sc.

Rnd 3: Ch 1, 2 sc in first sc, sc in next 3 sc, 2 sc in each of next 2 sc, sc in next 3 sc, 2 sc in last sc; join with slip st to first sc: 14 sc.

Rnd 4: Ch 1, 2 sc in first sc, sc in next 5 sc, 2 sc in each of next 2 sc, sc in next 5 sc, 2 sc in last sc; join with slip st to first sc: 18 sc.

Rnd 5: Ch 1, 2 sc in first sc, sc in next 7 sc, 2 sc in each of next 2 sc, sc in next 7 sc, 2 sc in last sc; join with slip st to first sc: 22 sc.

Rnd 6: Ch 1, 2 sc in first sc, sc in next 9 sc, 2 sc in each of next 2 sc, sc in next 9 sc, 2 sc in last sc; join with slip st to first sc: 26 sc.

Rnds 7-14: Ch 1, sc in each sc around; join with slip st to first sc.

Rnd 15: Ch 1, work beginning decrease, sc in next 9 sc, decrease twice, sc in next 9 sc, work ending decrease; join with slip st to first sc: 22 sc.

Rnd 16: Ch 1, work beginning decrease, sc in next 7 sc, decrease twice, sc in next 7 sc, work ending decrease; join with slip st to first sc: 18 sc.

Rnd 17: Ch 1, work beginning decrease, sc in next 5 sc, decrease twice, sc in next 5 sc, work ending decrease; join with slip st to first sc: 14 sc.

Rnd 18: Ch 1, work beginning decrease, sc in next 3 sc, decrease twice, sc in next 3 sc, work ending decrease; join with slip st to first sc: 10 sc.

Rnd 19: Ch 1, work beginning decrease, sc in next sc, decrease twice, sc in next sc, work ending decrease; join with slip st to first sc: 6 sc.

Rnd 20: Ch 1, pull up a loop in first 3 sc, YO and draw through all 4 loops on hook, pull up a loop in last 3 sc, YO and draw through all 4 loops on hook; join with slip st to first st, finish off.

Using photo as a guide for placement, sew Stems together, then sew Leaves to Stems.

Glue magnets to wrong side.

HALF CIRCLE RUG

Shown on page 39.

Finished Size: 19"w x 37"l
(48.5 cm x 94 cm)

MATERIALS
Bulky Weight Cotton Yarn:
  Red - 10 ounces, 170 yards
    (280 grams, 155.5 meters)
  Black - 6 ounces, 100 yards
    (170 grams, 91.5 meters)
  White - 4 ounces, 70 yards
    (110 grams, 64 meters)
Crochet hook, size P (10 mm) **or** size
  needed for gauge

GAUGE: 7 dc = 4" (10 cm);
        3 rows = 3$\frac{1}{4}$" (8.25 cm)

Gauge Swatch: 4" x 3$\frac{1}{4}$" (10 cm x 8.25 cm)
With Red, ch 9.
Row 1: Dc in fourth ch from hook
(3 skipped chs count as first dc) and
in each ch across: 7 dc.
Rows 2 and 3: Ch 3 **(counts as first
dc)**, turn; dc in next dc and in each dc
across.
Finish off.

RUG BODY
With Black, ch 28.

Row 1 (Right side): Sc in second ch from
hook, hdc in next ch, dc in next ch
changing to White **(Fig. 5, page 94)**, dc in
next 3 chs changing to Black in last dc
made, ★ dc in next 3 chs changing to
White in last dc made, dc in next 3 chs
changing to Black in last dc made; repeat
from ★ across to last 3 chs, dc in next ch,
hdc in next ch, sc in last ch; do **not**
change color: 27 sts.

Note: Loop a short piece of yarn around
any stitch to mark Row 1 as **right** side.

Continue to change colors in same
manner.

Row 2: Ch 4, turn; sc in second ch from
hook, hdc in next ch, dc in next ch, with
White dc in next 3 sts, ★ with Black dc in
next 3 dc, with White dc in next 3 sts;
repeat from ★ across, with Black add on
one dc **(Fig. 8, page 94)**, add on one hdc
(Fig. 7, page 94), add on one sc **(Fig. 6,
page 94)**; do **not** change color: 33 sts.

Row 3: Ch 4, turn; sc in second ch from
hook, hdc in next ch, dc in next ch, with
White dc in next 3 sts, ★ with Black dc in
next 3 dc, with White dc in next 3 sts;
repeat from ★ across, with Black add on
(dc, hdc, sc); do **not** change color: 39 sts.

Row 4: Ch 4, turn; sc in second ch from
hook, hdc in next ch, dc in next ch, with
White dc in next 3 sts, with Black dc in
next 3 dc, do **not** work over Black and
White, with Red dc in next 27 dc, with
second Black dc in next 3 dc, with second
White dc in last 3 sts, with Black add on
(dc, hdc, sc); do **not** change color: 45 sts.

Row 5: Ch 4, turn; sc in second ch from
hook, hdc in next ch, dc in next ch, with
White dc in next 3 sts, with Black dc in
next 3 dc, with Red dc in next 33 dc, with
Black dc in next 3 dc, with White dc in
last 3 sts, with Black add on (dc, hdc, sc);
do **not** change color: 51 sts.

Row 6: Ch 4, turn; sc in second ch from
hook, hdc in next ch, dc in next ch, with
White dc in next 3 sts, with Black dc in
next 3 dc, with Red dc in next 39 dc, with
Black dc in next 3 dc, with White dc in
last 3 sts, with Black add on (dc, hdc, sc);
do **not** change color: 57 sts.

Continued on page 38.

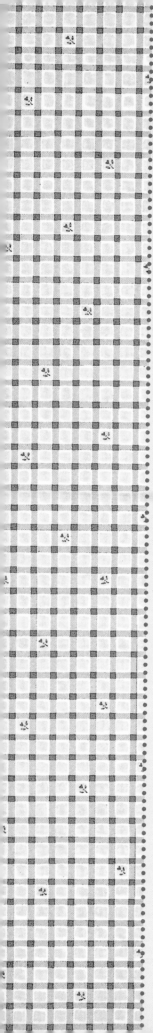

Row 7: Ch 4, turn; sc in second ch from hook, hdc in next ch, dc in next ch, with White dc in next 3 sts, with Black dc in next 3 dc, with Red dc in next 45 dc, with Black dc in next 3 dc, with White dc in last 3 sts, with Black add on (dc, hdc, sc) changing to White: 63 sts.

Row 8: Ch 3, turn; dc in next 2 sts, with Black dc in next 3 dc, with White dc in next 3 dc, with Red dc in next 45 dc, with White dc in next 3 dc, with Black dc in last 3 dc, with White dc in last 3 sts, changing to Black.

Row 9: Ch 3, turn; dc in next 2 dc, with White dc in next 3 dc, with Black dc in next 3 dc, with Red dc in next 45 dc, with Black dc in next 3 dc, with White dc in next 3 dc, with Black dc in last 3 dc.

Row 10: Ch 3, turn; dc in next 2 dc, with Black dc in next 3 dc, with White dc in next 3 dc, with Red dc in next 45 dc, with White dc in next 3 dc, with Black dc in next 3 dc, with White dc in last 3 dc.

Rows 11-14: Repeat Rows 9 and 10 twice; at end of Row 14 cut first Black, first White, and Red.

Row 15: Ch 3, turn; dc in next 2 dc, ★ with White dc in next 3 dc, with Black dc in next 3 dc; repeat from ★ across.

Row 16: Ch 3, turn; dc in next 2 dc, ★ with Black dc in next 3 dc, with White dc in next 3 dc; repeat from ★ across.

Row 17: Ch 3, turn; dc in next 2 dc, ★ with White dc in next 3 dc, with Black dc in next 3 dc; repeat from ★ across; cut White only.

EDGING

Rnd 1: Ch 1, do **not** turn; sc evenly around working 3 sc in each corner; join with slip st to first sc, finish off.

Rnd 2: With **right** side facing, join Red with slip st in any sc; ch 1, working from **left** to **right**, work reverse sc in same st and in each sc around (**Figs. 9a-d, page 94**); join with slip st to first st, finish off.

"Sow good services; sweet remembrances will grow from them."

– Mde. de Stael

RECTANGULAR RUG

Shown on page 41.

Finished Size: 25"w x 37"l
(63.5 cm x 94 cm)

MATERIALS
Bulky Weight Cotton Yarn:
Red - 18½ ounces, 315 yards
(530 grams, 288 meters)
Black - 7½ ounces, 130 yards
(210 grams, 119 meters)
White - 6½ ounces, 110 yards
(180 grams, 100.5 meters)
Crochet hook, size P (10 mm) **or** size needed for gauge
Yarn needle

GAUGE: 7 dc = 4" (10 cm);
3 rows = 3¼" (8.25 cm)

Gauge Swatch: 4" x 3¼" (10 cm x 8.25 cm)
With Red, ch 9.
Row 1: Dc in fourth ch from hook **(3 skipped chs count as first dc)** and in each ch across: 7 dc.
Rows 2 and 3: Ch 3 **(counts as first dc, now and throughout)**, turn; dc in next dc and in each dc across.
Finish off.

RUG BODY
With Black, ch 65.

Row 1 (Right side): Dc in fourth ch from hook **(3 skipped chs count as first dc)** and in next ch changing to White in last dc made **(Fig. 5, page 94)**, ★ dc in next 3 chs changing to Black in last dc made, dc in next 3 chs changing to White in last dc made; repeat from ★ across: 63 dc.

Note: Loop a short piece of yarn around any dc to mark Row 1 as **right** side.

Continue to change colors in same manner.

Row 2: Ch 3 **(counts as first dc, now and throughout)**, turn; dc in next 2 dc, ★ with Black dc in next 3 dc, with White dc in next 3 dc; repeat from ★ across.

Row 3: Ch 3, turn; dc in next 2 dc, ★ with White dc in next 3 dc, with Black dc in next 3 dc; repeat from ★ across.

Row 4: Ch 3, turn; dc in next 2 dc, with Black dc in next 3 dc, with White dc in next 3 dc, do **not** work over Black and White with Red dc in next 45 dc, with second White dc in next 3 dc, with second Black dc in next 3 dc, with White dc in last 3 dc.

Row 5: Ch 3, turn; dc in next 2 dc, with White dc in next 3 dc, with Black dc in next 3 dc; with Red dc in next 45 dc, with Black dc in next 3 dc, with White dc in next 3 dc, with Black dc in last 3 dc.

Rows 6-20: Repeat Rows 4 and 5, 7 times; then repeat Row 4 once **more**; at end of Row 20, cut first Black, first White, and Red.

Row 21: Ch 3, turn; dc in next 2 dc, ★ with White dc in next 3 dc, with Black dc in next 3 dc; repeat from ★ across.

Row 22: Ch 3, turn; dc in next 2 dc, ★ with Black dc in next 3 dc, with White dc in next 3 dc; repeat from ★ across.

Row 23: Ch 3, turn; dc in next 2 dc, ★ with White dc in next 3 dc, with Black dc in next 3 dc; repeat from ★ across; finish off both colors.

EDGING

Rnd 1: With **right** side facing, join Red with sc in any dc *(see Joining With Sc, page 92)*; sc evenly around working 3 sc in each corner; join with slip st to first sc.

Rnd 2: Ch 1, working from **left** to **right**, work reverse sc in each sc around **(Figs. 9a-d, page 94)**; join with slip st to first st, finish off.

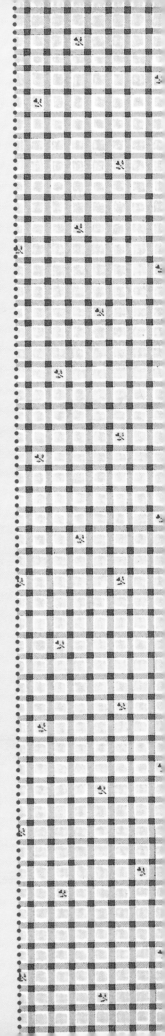

Cozy Den

Cheery colors and crocheted flowers make this darling den even more inviting. Drape a luxurious lemon throw over a sofa or favorite chair. Thick and warm with a lush fringe, it's the perfect wrap to snuggle up with. Scatter plump posy pillows around the room. In eye-catching shades and three distinct shapes, it would be practically impossible to have too many. A matching "fried-egg flower" rug in crimson and yellow makes a bold statement.

YELLOW AFGHAN

Shown on Front Cover and page 43.

Finished Size: 48" x 64"
(122 cm x 162.5 cm)

MATERIALS
Worsted Weight Yarn:
56 ounces, 3,120 yards
(1,590 grams, 2,853 meters)
Crochet hook, size H (5 mm) **or** size
needed for gauge
Yarn needle

GAUGE: Cluster, (ch 1, Cluster) 5 times
and 9 rows = 3¹/₄" (8.25 cm)

Gauge Swatch: 3³/₄" (9.5 cm) square
Ch 14.
Work same as Afghan Body for 11 rows.
Finish off.

STITCH GUIDE

BEGINNING CLUSTER
Pull up a loop in first sc and in next
ch-1 sp, YO and draw through all
3 loops on hook.

CLUSTER
Pull up a loop in next Cluster and in
next ch-1 sp, YO and draw through all
3 loops on hook.

AFGHAN BODY
Ch 162 **loosely**.

Row 1 (Right side): Pull up a loop in
second ch from hook and in next ch, YO
and draw through all 3 loops on hook
(beginning Cluster made), ch 1, ★ pull
up a loop in next 2 chs, YO and draw
through all 3 loops on hook **(Cluster
made)**, ch 1; repeat from ★ across to last
ch, sc in last ch: 80 Clusters, 80 ch-1 sps,
and one sc.

Note: Loop a short piece of yarn around
any stitch to mark Row 1 as **right** side.

Rows 2-178: Ch 1, turn; work
beginning Cluster, ch 1, (work Cluster,
ch 1) across to last Cluster, sc in last
Cluster; at end of Row 178, finish off.

FRINGE
Cut a piece of cardboard 5" (12.5 cm)
wide and 8" (20.5 cm) long. Wind the yarn
loosely and **evenly** lengthwise around
the cardboard until the card is filled, then
cut across one end; repeat as needed.
Hold together 3 strands of yarn; fold in
half.
With **wrong** side facing and using a
crochet hook, draw the folded end up
through a stitch and pull the loose ends
through the folded end **(Fig. 1a)**; draw
the knot up **tightly (Fig. 1b)**. Repeat in
every other stitch across short edges of
Afghan.
Lay flat on a hard surface and trim the
ends.

Fig. 1a

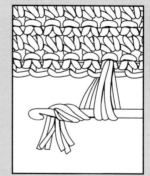

Fig. 1b

44

FLOWER PILLOW #1

Shown on Front Cover and page 43.

Finished Size: 14" (35.5 cm) diameter without Leaves

MATERIALS

Worsted Weight Yarn:

Orange - 8 ounces, 445 yards (230 grams, 407 meters)

Green - 6 ounces, 335 yards (170 grams, 306.5 meters)

Yellow - 3 ounces, 165 yards (90 grams, 151 meters)

Crochet hook, size H (5 mm) **or** size needed for gauge

2 - 7" (15 cm) diameter fabric circles

4 - 10" (25.5 cm) fabric squares

Polyester fiberfill

Sewing needle and thread

Yarn needle

GAUGE SWATCH: 2" (5 cm) diameter Work same as Rnds 1-4 of Center Back.

STITCH GUIDE

BEGINNING DECREASE

Pull up a loop in same st and in next sc, YO and draw through all 3 loops on hook **(counts as one sc).**

DECREASE

Pull up a loop in next 2 sc, YO and draw through all 3 loops on hook **(counts as one sc).**

ENDING DECREASE

Pull up a loop in last 2 sc, YO and draw through all 3 loops on hook **(counts as one sc).**

PILLOW FORMS

CENTER

With **right** sides of fabric circles together and using a 1/4" (7 mm) seam, sew circles together, leaving a 2" (5 cm) opening. Clip curves close to seam. Turn form right side out. Stuff firmly with polyester fiberfill and sew opening closed.

LEAVES

Using diagram as a guide, draw pattern onto a sheet of paper or newsprint. Pin pattern to fabric squares; then cut out Leaf.

With **right** sides of fabric together and using a 1/4" (7 mm) seam, sew fabric pieces together, leaving a 2" (5 cm) opening. Turn form right side out. Stuff firmly with polyester fiberfill and sew opening closed.

DIAGRAM

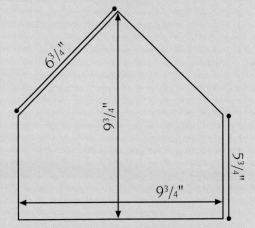

CENTER
BACK

Rnds 1-12: Work same as Flower Pillow #3 Center, page 51: 72 sc.

Rnd 13: Ch 1, 2 sc in same st, sc in next 11 sc, (2 sc in next sc, sc in next 11 sc) around; join with slip st to first sc: 78 sc.

Continued on page 46.

Rnd 14: Ch 1, sc in next 12 sc, 2 sc in next sc, (sc in next 12 sc, 2 sc in next sc) around; join with slip st to first sc: 84 sc.

Rnd 15: Ch 1, 2 sc in same st, sc in next 13 sc, (2 sc in next sc, sc in next 13 sc) around; join with slip st to first sc: 90 sc.

Rnd 16: Ch 1, sc in same st and in next 6 sc, 2 sc in next sc, (sc in next 14 sc, 2 sc in next sc) around to last 7 sc, sc in last 7 sc; join with slip st to first sc: 96 sc.

Rnd 17: Ch 1, sc in same st and in next 14 sc, 2 sc in next sc, (sc in next 15 sc, 2 sc in next sc) around; join with slip st to first sc, finish off: 102 sc.

FRONT
Rnds 1-17: Work same as Center Back; do **not** finish off: 102 sc.

Joining Rnd: Ch 1, with **wrong** sides of Centers together, Front facing, and working through **inside** loops only; slip st in same st and in each sc around inserting Center pillow form before closing; join with slip st to first slip st, finish off.

BODY
FRONT
Rnd 1: With Center Front facing and working in free loops of sc on Rnd 17 (**Fig. 3a, page 93**), join Orange with sc in same st as joining (**see Joining With Sc, page 92**); sc in next 15 sc, 2 sc in next sc, (sc in next 16 sc, 2 sc in next sc) around; join with slip st to first sc: 108 sc.

Rnd 2: Ch 1, sc in same st and in next 8 sc, 2 sc in next sc, (sc in next 17 sc, 2 sc in next sc) around to last 8 sc, sc in last 8 sc; join with slip st to first sc: 114 sc.

Rnd 3: Ch 1, sc in same st and in next 17 sc, 2 sc in next sc, (sc in next 18 sc, 2 sc in next sc) around; join with slip st to first sc: 120 sc.

Rnd 4: Ch 1, 2 sc in same st, sc in next 19 sc, (2 sc in next sc, sc in next 19 sc) around; join with slip st to first sc: 126 sc.

Rnd 5: Ch 1, sc in same st and in next 9 sc, 2 sc in next sc, (sc in next 20 sc, 2 sc in next sc) around to last 10 sc, sc in last 10 sc; join with slip st to first sc: 132 sc.

Rnd 6: Ch 1, sc in same st and in next 20 sc, 2 sc in next sc, (sc in next 21 sc, 2 sc in next sc) around; join with slip st to first sc: 138 sc.

Rnd 7: Ch 1, 2 sc in same st, sc in next 22 sc, (2 sc in next sc, sc in next 22 sc) around; join with slip st to first sc: 144 sc.

Rnd 8: Ch 1, sc in same st and in next 11 sc, 2 sc in next sc, (sc in next 23 sc, 2 sc in next sc) around to last 11 sc, sc in last 11 sc; join with slip st to first sc: 150 sc.

Rnd 9: Ch 1, sc in same st and in next 23 sc, 2 sc in next sc, (sc in next 24 sc, 2 sc in next sc) around; join with slip st to first sc: 156 sc.

Rnd 10: Ch 1, 2 sc in same st, sc in next 25 sc, (2 sc in next sc, sc in next 25 sc) around; join with slip st to first sc: 162 sc.

Rnd 11: Ch 1, sc in same st and in next 12 sc, 2 sc in next sc, (sc in next 26 sc, 2 sc in next sc) around to last 13 sc, sc in last 13 sc; join with slip st to first sc; do **not** finish off: 168 sc.

FIRST PETAL
Row 1: Ch 1, sc in same st and in next 20 sc, leave remaining 147 sc unworked: 21 sc.

Rows 2-8: Ch 1, turn; sc in each sc across.

Finish off.

SECOND THRU SEVENTH PETAL

Row 1: With **right** side facing, join Orange with sc in next sc on Rnd 11 of Body; sc in next 20 sc, leave remaining sc unworked: 21 sc.

Rows 2-8: Ch 1, turn; sc in each sc across.

Finish off.

LAST PETAL

Row 1: With **right** side facing, join Orange with sc in next sc on Rnd 11 of Body; sc in last 20 sc: 21 sc.

Rows 2-8: Ch 1, turn; sc in each sc across; do **not** finish off.

EDGING

Ch 1, turn; ★ 3 sc in first sc, sc in next 19 sc, 3 sc in last sc; working in end of rows, skip first row, sc in next 14 rows, skip last row; repeat from ★ around; join with slip st to first sc, finish off: 312 sc.

BACK

Rnd 1: With Center Back facing and working in free loops of sc on Rnd 17, join Orange with sc in sc before joining; sc in next 15 sc, 2 sc in next sc, (sc in next 16 sc, 2 sc in next sc) around; join with slip st to first sc: 108 sc.

Complete same as Body Front.

LEAF (Make 2)

With Green, ch 37.

Row 1 (Right side)**:** Sc in second ch from hook and in each ch across: 36 sc.

Note: Loop a short piece of yarn around any sc to mark Row 1 as **right** side.

Rows 2-10: Ch 1, turn; sc in each sc across.

Begin working in rounds.

Rnd 1: Ch 1, turn; working in Front Loops Only (**Fig. 2, *page* 93**), sc in each sc across; **turn**; working in free loops of same sc, sc in each sc across; join with slip st to **both** loops of first sc: 72 sc.

Rnds 2-20: Ch 1, do **not** turn; working in both loops, sc in each sc around; join with slip st to first sc.

Rnd 21: Ch 1, work beginning decrease, sc in next 32 sc, decrease twice, sc in next 32 sc, work ending decrease; join with slip st to first sc: 68 sc.

Rnd 22: Ch 1, work beginning decrease, sc in next 30 sc, decrease twice, sc in next 30 sc, work ending decrease; join with slip st to first sc: 64 sc.

Rnd 23: Ch 1, work beginning decrease, sc in next 28 sc, decrease twice, sc in next 28 sc, work ending decrease; join with slip st to first sc: 60 sc.

Rnd 24: Ch 1, work beginning decrease, sc in next 26 sc, decrease twice, sc in next 26 sc, work ending decrease; join with slip st to first sc: 56 sc.

Rnd 25: Ch 1, work beginning decrease, sc in next 24 sc, decrease twice, sc in next 24 sc, work ending decrease; join with slip st to first sc: 52 sc.

Rnd 26: Ch 1, work beginning decrease, sc in next 22 sc, decrease twice, sc in next 22 sc, work ending decrease; join with slip st to first sc: 48 sc.

Rnd 27: Ch 1, work beginning decrease, sc in next 20 sc, decrease twice, sc in next 20 sc, work ending decrease; join with slip st to first sc: 44 sc.

Rnd 28: Ch 1, work beginning decrease, sc in next 18 sc, decrease twice, sc in next 18 sc, work ending decrease; join with slip st to first sc: 40 sc.

Continued on page 48.

Rnd 29: Ch 1, work beginning decrease, sc in next 16 sc, decrease twice, sc in next 16 sc, work ending decrease; join with slip st to first sc: 36 sc.

Rnd 30: Ch 1, work beginning decrease, sc in next 14 sc, decrease twice, sc in next 14 sc, work ending decrease; join with slip st to first sc: 32 sc.

Rnd 31: Ch 1, work beginning decrease, sc in next 12 sc, decrease twice, sc in next 12 sc, work ending decrease; join with slip st to first sc: 28 sc.

Rnd 32: Ch 1, work beginning decrease, sc in next 10 sc, decrease twice, sc in next 10 sc, work ending decrease; join with slip st to first sc: 24 sc.

Rnd 33: Ch 1, work beginning decrease, sc in next 8 sc, decrease twice, sc in next 8 sc, work ending decrease; join with slip st to first sc: 20 sc.

Rnd 34: Ch 1, work beginning decrease, sc in next 6 sc, decrease twice, sc in next 6 sc, work ending decrease; join with slip st to first sc: 16 sc.

Insert Leaf pillow form.

Rnd 35: Ch 1, work beginning decrease, sc in next 4 sc, decrease twice, sc in next 4 sc, work ending decrease; join with slip st to first sc: 12 sc.

Rnd 36: Ch 1, work beginning decrease, sc in next 2 sc, decrease twice, sc in next 2 sc, work ending decrease; join with slip st to first sc: 8 sc.

Rnd 37: Ch 1, work beginning decrease, decrease twice, work ending decrease; join with slip st to first sc, finish off leaving a long end for sewing: 4 sc.

Thread yarn needle with long end, weave through stitches on Rnd 37, gather tightly and secure end.

Using photo as a guide for placement, pin Leaves in place at Row 10 between Front and Back of Body, then sew through **all** thicknesses around entire Body stuffing with polyester fiberfill before closing.

FLOWER PILLOW #2

Shown on Front Cover and page 43.

Finished Size: 14" (35.5 cm) diameter without Leaves

MATERIALS
Worsted Weight Yarn:
    Red - 9 ounces, 500 yards
        (260 grams, 457 meters)
    Yellow - 7½ ounces, 420 yards
        (210 grams, 384 meters)
    Green - 5 ounces, 280 yards
        (140 grams, 256 meters)

Crochet hook, size H (5 mm) **or** size
    needed for gauge
2 - 15" (38 cm) diameter fabric circles
4 - 10" (25.5 cm) fabric squares
Polyester fiberfill
Sewing needle and thread
Yarn needle

GAUGE SWATCH: 2" (5 cm) diameter
Work same as Rnds 1-4 of Center, page 49.

STITCH GUIDE

BEGINNING DECREASE
Pull up a loop in same st and in next sc, YO and draw through all 3 loops on hook (counts as one sc).

DECREASE
Pull up a loop in next 2 sc, YO and draw through all 3 loops on hook (counts as one sc).

ENDING DECREASE
Pull up a loop in last 2 sc, YO and draw through all 3 loops on hook (counts as one sc).

PILLOW FORMS

CENTER
With **right** sides of fabric circles together and using a ¹/₄" (7 mm) seam, sew circles together, leaving a 2" (5 cm) opening. Clip curves close to seam. Turn form right side out. Stuff firmly with polyester fiberfill and sew opening closed.

LEAVES
Using diagram, page 95 as a guide, draw pattern onto a sheet of paper or newsprint. Pin pattern to fabric squares; then cut out Leaf.

With **right** sides of fabric together and using a ¹/₄" (7 mm) seam, sew fabric pieces together, leaving a 2" (5 cm) opening. Turn form right side out. Stuff firmly with polyester fiberfill and sew opening closed.

CENTER (Make 2)

Rnds 1-12: Work same as Flower Pillow #3 Center, page 51: 72 sc.

Rnd 13: Ch 1, 2 sc in same st, sc in next 11 sc, (2 sc in next sc, sc in next 11 sc) around; join with slip st to first sc: 78 sc.

Rnd 14: Ch 1, sc in same st and in next 11 sc, 2 sc in next sc, (sc in next 12 sc, 2 sc in next sc) around; join with slip st to first sc: 84 sc.

Rnd 15: Ch 1, 2 sc in same st, sc in next 13 sc, (2 sc in next sc, sc in next 13 sc) around; join with slip st to first sc: 90 sc.

Rnd 16: Ch 1, sc in same st and in next 6 sc, 2 sc in next sc, (sc in next 14 sc, 2 sc in next sc) around to last 7 sc, sc in last 7 sc; join with slip st to first sc: 96 sc.

Rnd 17: Ch 1, sc in same st and in next 14 sc, 2 sc in next sc, (sc in next 15 sc, 2 sc in next sc) around; join with slip st to first sc: 102 sc.

Rnd 18: Ch 1, 2 sc in same st, sc in next 16 sc, (2 sc in next sc, sc in next 16 sc) around; join with slip st to first sc: 108 sc.

Rnd 19: Ch 1, sc in same st and in next 8 sc, 2 sc in next sc, (sc in next 17 sc, 2 sc in next sc) around to last 8 sc, sc in last 8 sc; join with slip st to first sc: 114 sc.

Rnd 20: Ch 1, sc in same st and in next 17 sc, 2 sc in next sc, (sc in next 18 sc, 2 sc in next sc) around; join with slip st to first sc: 120 sc.

Rnd 21: Ch 1, 2 sc in same st, sc in next 19 sc, (2 sc in next sc, sc in next 19 sc) around; join with slip st to first sc: 126 sc.

Rnd 22: Ch 1, sc in same st and in next 9 sc, 2 sc in next sc, (sc in next 20 sc, 2 sc in next sc) around to last 10 sc, sc in last 10 sc; join with slip st to first sc: 132 sc.

Rnd 23: Ch 1, sc in same st and in next 20 sc, 2 sc in next sc, (sc in next 21 sc, 2 sc in next sc) around; join with slip st to first sc: 138 sc.

Continued on page 50.

Rnd 24: Ch 1, 2 sc in same st, sc in next 22 sc, (2 sc in next sc, sc in next 22 sc) around; join with slip st to first sc: 144 sc.

Rnd 25: Ch 1, sc in same st and in next 11 sc, 2 sc in next sc, (sc in next 23 sc, 2 sc in next sc) around to last 11 sc, sc in last 11 sc; join with slip st to first sc: 150 sc.

Rnd 26: Ch 1, sc in same st and in next 23 sc, 2 sc in next sc, (sc in next 24 sc, 2 sc in next sc) around; join with slip st to first sc, finish off: 156 sc.

Rnd 27: With **right** side facing, join Red with sc in same st as joining (***see Joining With Sc, page 92***); sc in same st, sc in next 25 sc, (2 sc in next sc, sc in next 25 sc) around; join with slip st to first sc: 162 sc.

Rnd 28: Ch 1, sc in same st and in next 12 sc, 2 sc in next sc, (sc in next 26 sc, 2 sc in next sc) around to last 13 sc, sc in last 13 sc; join with slip st to first sc: 168 sc.

Rnd 29: Ch 1, sc in same st and in next 26 sc, 2 sc in next sc, (sc in next 27 sc, 2 sc in next sc) around; join with slip st to first sc: 174 sc.

Rnd 30: Ch 1, 2 sc in same st, sc in next 28 sc, (2 sc in next sc, sc in next 28 sc) around; join with slip st to first sc, do **not** finish off: 180 sc.

FIRST PETAL

Row 1: Ch 1, turn; 2 sc in first sc, sc in next 18 sc, 2 sc in next sc, leave remaining 160 sc unworked: 22 sc.

Rows 2-15: Ch 1, turn; 2 sc in first sc, sc in each sc across to last sc, 2 sc in last sc: 50 sc.

Rows 16-20: Ch 1, turn; sc in each sc across.

Finish off.

SECOND PETAL

Row 1: With **wrong** side facing, skip next 40 sc from Petal just made and join Red with sc in next sc; sc in same st, sc in next 18 sc, 2 sc in next sc, leave remaining sc unworked: 22 sc.

Complete same as First Petal.

THIRD PETAL

Work same as Second Petal; do **not** finish off.

EDGING

Ch 1, turn; ★ 3 sc in first sc, sc in next 48 sc, 3 sc in last sc; sc in end of each row across; sc in next 40 skipped sc on Rnd 1; sc in end of each row across; repeat from ★ 2 times **more**; join with slip st to first sc, finish off.

LEAF (Make 2)

With Green, ch 37.

Foundation Row: Sc in second ch from hook and in each ch across: 36 sc.

Complete same as Flower Pillow #1 Leaf, page 47.

FINISHING

Using diagram, page 95 as a guide:

Working through **both** thicknesses of Row 1 of Petals and in skipped sc on Edging **between** Petals, sew around entire Center inserting pillow form before closing.

Matching rows, sew Front and Back Petals together along outer edges leaving sc on Row 20 unsewn.

Fold Petals over Center and sew in place.

Using photo as a guide for placement, sew Leaves in place along outer edge.

FLOWER PILLOW #3

Shown on Front Cover and page 43.

Finished Size: 14" (35.5 cm) diameter without Leaves

MATERIALS

Worsted Weight Yarn:

Blue - 7½ ounces, 420 yards (210 grams, 384 meters)

Green - 5 ounces, 280 yards (140 grams, 256 meters)

Yellow - 3 ounces, 165 yards (90 grams, 151 meters)

Crochet hook, size H (5 mm) **or** size needed for gauge

2 - 8" (15 cm) diameter fabric circles

4 - 10" (25.5 cm) fabric squares

Polyester fiberfill

Sewing needle and thread

Yarn needle

GAUGE SWATCH: 2" (5 cm) diameter

Work same as Rnds 1-4 of Center Back.

STITCH GUIDE

BEGINNING DECREASE

Pull up a loop in same st and in next sc, YO and draw through all 3 loops on hook **(counts as one sc)**.

DECREASE

Pull up a loop in next 2 sc, YO and draw through all 3 loops on hook **(counts as one sc)**.

ENDING DECREASE

Pull up a loop in last 2 sc, YO and draw through all 3 loops on hook **(counts as one sc)**.

PILLOW FORMS

CENTER

With **right** sides of fabric circles together and using a ¼" (7 mm) seam, sew circles together, leaving a 2" (5 cm) opening. Clip curves close to seam. Turn form right side out. Stuff firmly with polyester fiberfill and sew opening closed.

LEAVES

Using diagram, page 54, as a guide, draw pattern onto a sheet of paper or newsprint. Pin pattern to remaining fabric squares; then cut out Leaf.

With **right** sides of fabric together and using a ¼" (7 mm) seam, sew fabric pieces together, leaving a 2" (5 cm) opening. Turn form right side out. Stuff firmly with polyester fiberfill and sew opening closed.

CENTER

BACK

Rnd 1 (Right side): With Yellow, ch 2, 6 sc in second ch from hook; join with slip st to first sc.

Note: Loop a short piece of yarn around any sc to mark Rnd 1 as **right** side.

Rnd 2: Ch 1, 2 sc in same st and in each sc around; join with slip st to first sc: 12 sc.

Rnd 3: Ch 1, sc in same st, 2 sc in next sc, (sc in next sc, 2 sc in next sc) around; join with slip st to first sc: 18 sc.

Rnd 4: Ch 1, 2 sc in same st, sc in next 2 sc, (2 sc in next sc, sc in next 2 sc) around; join with slip st to first sc: 24 sc.

Continued on page 52.

Rnd 5: Ch 1, sc in same st and in next 2 sc, 2 sc in next sc, (sc in next 3 sc, 2 sc in next sc) around; join with slip st to first sc: 30 sc.

Rnd 6: Ch 1, 2 sc in same st, sc in next 4 sc, (2 sc in next sc, sc in next 4 sc) around; join with slip st to first sc: 36 sc.

Rnd 7: Ch 1, sc in same st and in next 4 sc, 2 sc in next sc, (sc in next 5 sc, 2 sc in next sc) around; join with slip st to first sc: 42 sc.

Rnd 8: Ch 1, 2 sc in same st, sc in next 6 sc, (2 sc in next sc, sc in next 6 sc) around; join with slip st to first sc: 48 sc.

Rnd 9: Ch 1, sc in same st and in next 6 sc, 2 sc in next sc, (sc in next 7 sc, 2 sc in next sc) around; join with slip st to first sc: 54 sc.

Rnd 10: Ch 1, sc in same st and in next 3 sc, 2 sc in next sc, (sc in next 8 sc, 2 sc in next sc) around to last 4 sc, sc in last 4 sc; join with slip st to first sc: 60 sc.

Rnd 11: Ch 1, sc in same st and in next 8 sc, 2 sc in next sc, (sc in next 9 sc, 2 sc in next sc) around; join with slip st to first sc: 66 sc.

Rnd 12: Ch 1, sc in same st and in next 4 sc, 2 sc in next sc, (sc in next 10 sc, 2 sc in next sc) around to last 5 sc, sc in last 5 sc; join with slip st to first sc: 72 sc.

Rnd 13: Ch 1, 2 sc in same st, sc in next 11 sc, (2 sc in next sc, sc in next 11 sc) around; join with slip st to first sc, finish off: 78 sc.

FRONT

Work same as Back; do **not** finish off: 78 sc.

Joining Rnd: Ch 1, with **wrong** sides of Centers together, Front facing, and working through **inside** loops only, slip st in same st and in each sc around inserting Center pillow form before closing; join with slip st to first slip st, finish off.

BODY
FRONT

Rnd 1: With **right** side facing and working in free loops of Rnd 13 **(Fig. 3a, page 93)**, join Blue with sc in same st as joining **(see Joining With Sc, page 92)**; sc in next 11 sc, 2 sc in next sc, (sc in next 12 sc, 2 sc in next sc) around; join with slip st to first sc: 84 sc.

Rnd 2: Ch 1, 2 sc in same st, sc in next 13 sc, (2 sc in next sc, sc in next 13 sc) around; join with slip st to first sc: 90 sc.

Rnd 3: Ch 1, sc in same st and in next 6 sc, 2 sc in next sc, (sc in next 14 sc, 2 sc in next sc) around to last 7 sc, sc in last 7 sc; join with slip st to first sc: 96 sc.

Rnd 4: Ch 1, sc in same st and in next 14 sc, 2 sc in next sc, (sc in next 15 sc, 2 sc in next sc) around; join with slip st to first sc: 102 sc.

Rnd 5: Ch 1, 2 sc in same st, sc in next 16 sc, (2 sc in next sc, sc in next 16 sc) around; join with slip st to first sc: 108 sc.

Rnd 6: Ch 1, sc in same st and in next 8 sc, 2 sc in next sc, (sc in next 17 sc, 2 sc in next sc) around to last 8 sc, sc in last 8 sc; join with slip st to first sc: 114 sc.

Rnd 7: Ch 1, sc in same st and in next 17 sc, 2 sc in next sc, (sc in next 18 sc, 2 sc in next sc) around; join with slip st to first sc: 120 sc.

Rnd 8: Ch 1, 2 sc in same st, sc in next 19 sc, (2 sc in next sc, sc in next 19 sc) around; join with slip st to first sc: 126 sc.

Rnd 9: Ch 1, sc in same st and in next 9 sc, 2 sc in next sc, (sc in next 20 sc, 2 sc in next sc) around to last 10 sc, sc in last 10 sc; join with slip st to first sc: 132 sc.

Rnd 10: Ch 1, sc in same st and in next 20 sc, 2 sc in next sc, (sc in next 21 sc, 2 sc in next sc) around; join with slip st to first sc: 138 sc.

Rnd 11: Ch 1, 2 sc in same st, sc in next 22 sc, (2 sc in next sc, sc in next 22 sc) around; join with slip st to first sc: 144 sc.

Rnd 12: Ch 1, sc in same st and in next 11 sc, 2 sc in next sc, (sc in next 23 sc, 2 sc in next sc) around to last 11 sc, sc in last 11 sc; join with slip st to first sc: 150 sc.

Rnd 13: Ch 1, sc in same st and in next 23 sc, 2 sc in next sc, (sc in next 24 sc, 2 sc in next sc) around; join with slip st to first sc: 156 sc.

Rnd 14: Ch 1, 2 sc in same st, sc in next 25 sc, (2 sc in next sc, sc in next 25 sc) around; join with slip st to first sc: 162 sc.

Rnd 15: Ch 1, sc in same st and in next 12 sc, 2 sc in next sc, (sc in next 26 sc, 2 sc in next sc) around to last 13 sc, sc in last 13 sc; join with slip st to first sc: 168 sc.

Rnd 16: Ch 1, sc in same st and in next 26 sc, 2 sc in next sc, (sc in next 27 sc, 2 sc in next sc) around; join with slip st to first sc: 174 sc.

Rnd 17: Ch 1, 2 sc in same st, sc in next 28 sc, (2 sc in next sc, sc in next 28 sc) around; join with slip st to first sc: 180 sc.

Rnd 18: Ch 1, sc in same st and in next 14 sc, 2 sc in next sc, (sc in next 29 sc, 2 sc in next sc) around to last 14 sc, sc in last 14 sc; join with slip st to first sc: 186 sc.

Rnd 19: Ch 1, sc in same st and in next 29 sc, 2 sc in next sc, (sc in next 30 sc, 2 sc in next sc) around; join with slip st to first sc: 192 sc.

Rnd 20: Ch 1, 2 sc in same st, sc in next 31 sc, (2 sc in next sc, sc in next 31 sc) around; join with slip st to first sc: 198 sc.

Rnd 21: Ch 1, sc in same st and in next 15 sc, 2 sc in next sc, (sc in next 32 sc, 2 sc in next sc) around to last 16 sc, sc in last 16 sc; join with slip st to first sc: 204 sc.

Rnd 22: Ch 1, sc in same st and in next 32 sc, 2 sc in next sc, (sc in next 33 sc, 2 sc in next sc) around; join with slip st to first sc: 210 sc.

Rnd 23: Ch 1, 2 sc in same st, sc in next 34 sc, (2 sc in next sc, sc in next 34 sc) around; join with slip st to first sc, finish off: 216 sc.

BACK
Work same as Body Front.

LEAF (Make 2)
With Green, ch 37.

Foundation Row: Sc in second ch from hook and in each ch across: 36 sc.

Rnd 1: Ch 1, turn; working in Front Loops Only (**Fig. 2, *page 92***), sc in each sc across; **turn**; working in free loops of same sc, sc in each sc across; join with slip st to **both** loops of first sc: 72 sc.

53

Continued on page 54.

Rnds 2-21: Ch 1, do **not** turn; working in both loops, sc in same st and in each sc around; join with slip st to first sc.

Rnd 22: Ch 1, work beginning decrease, sc in next 32 sc, decrease twice, sc in next 32 sc, work ending decrease; join with slip st to first sc: 68 sc.

Rnd 23: Ch 1, sc in same st and in each sc around; join with slip st to first sc.

Rnd 24: Ch 1, work beginning decrease, sc in next 30 sc, decrease twice, sc in next 30 sc, work ending decrease; join with slip st to first sc: 64 sc.

Rnd 25: Ch 1, sc in same st and in each sc around; join with slip st to first sc.

Rnd 26: Ch 1, work beginning decrease, sc in next 28 sc, decrease twice, sc in next 28 sc, work ending decrease; join with slip st to first sc: 60 sc.

Rnd 27: Ch 1, sc in same st and in each sc around; join with slip st to first sc.

Rnd 28: Ch 1, work beginning decrease, sc in next 26 sc, decrease twice, sc in next 26 sc, work ending decrease; join with slip st to first sc: 56 sc.

Rnd 29: Ch 1, sc in same st and in each sc around; join with slip st to first sc.

Rnd 30: Ch 1, work beginning decrease, decrease, sc in next 20 sc, decrease 4 times, sc in next 20 sc, decrease, work ending decrease; join with slip st to first sc: 48 sc.

Rnd 31: Ch 1, sc in same st and in each sc around; join with slip st to first sc.

Rnd 32: Ch 1, work beginning decrease, decrease, sc in next 16 sc, decrease 4 times, sc in next 16 sc, decrease, work ending decrease; join with slip st to first sc: 40 sc.

Rnd 33: Ch 1, sc in same st and in each sc around; join with slip st to first sc.

Rnd 34: Ch 1, work beginning decrease, hdc in next 5 sc, dc in next 6 sc, hdc in next 5 sc, decrease twice, hdc in next 5 sc, dc in next 6 sc, hdc in next 5 sc, work ending decrease; join with slip st to first sc, finish off leaving a long end for sewing.

Insert each Leaf pillow form. Thread yarn needle with long end and sew opening closed.

Using photo as a guide for placement, pin Leaves in place between Front and Back of Body, then sew through **all** thicknesses around entire Body stuffing with polyester fiberfill before closing.

DIAGRAM

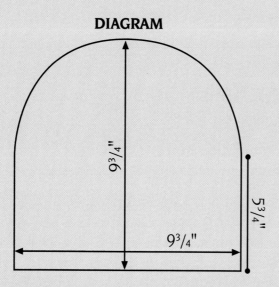

9³/4"

9³/4"

5³/4"

54

FLOWER RUG

Shown on Front Cover and pages 43 and 57.

Finished Size: 36" (91.5 cm) diameter

MATERIALS

Bulky Weight Cotton Yarn:
    Red - 34$\frac{1}{2}$ ounces, 580 yards
        (980 grams, 530.5 meters)
    Green - 13$\frac{1}{2}$ ounces, 230 yards
        (380 grams, 210.5 meters)
    Yellow - 4$\frac{1}{2}$ ounces, 80 yards
        (130 grams, 73 meters)
Crochet hook, size P (10 mm) **or** size
    needed for gauge

GAUGE SWATCH: 4" (10 cm) diameter
Work same as Rnds 1-3 of Center.

STITCH GUIDE

BEGINNING DECREASE
Pull up a loop in first 2 sc, YO and
draw through all 3 loops on hook
(counts as one sc).

ENDING DECREASE
Pull up a loop in last 2 sc, YO and
draw through all 3 loops on hook
(counts as one sc).

CENTER

Rnds 1-12: Work same as Flower Pillow
#3 Center, page 51: 72 sc.

Rnd 13: Ch 1, 2 sc in same st, sc in next
5 sc, (2 sc in next sc, sc in next 5 sc)
around; join with slip st to first sc,
finish off: 84 sc.

BODY

Rnd 1: With **right** side facing, join Red
with dc in same st as joining **(see Joining
With Dc, page 93)**; dc in next 5 sc, 2 dc
in next sc, (dc in next 6 sc, 2 dc in next
sc) around; join with slip st to first dc:
96 dc.

Rnd 2: Ch 3 **(counts as first dc, now
and throughout)**, dc in same st and in
next 7 dc, (2 dc in next dc, dc in next
7 dc) around; join with slip st to first dc:
108 dc.

Rnd 3: Ch 3, dc in next 3 dc, 2 dc in next
dc, (dc in next 8 dc, 2 dc in next dc)
around to last 4 dc, dc in last 4 dc; join
with slip st to first dc: 120 dc.

Rnd 4: Ch 3, dc in same st and in next
9 dc, (2 dc in next dc, dc in next 9 dc)
around; join with slip st to first dc:
132 dc.

Rnd 5: Ch 3, dc in next 9 dc, 2 dc in next
dc, (dc in next 10 dc, 2 dc in next dc)
around; join with slip st to first dc:
144 dc.

Rnd 6: Ch 3, dc in next 5 dc, 2 dc in next
dc, (dc in next 11 dc, 2 dc in next dc)
around to last 5 dc, dc in last 5 dc; join
with slip st to first dc: 156 dc.

Rnd 7: Ch 3, dc in same st and in next
12 dc, (2 dc in next dc, dc in next 12 dc)
around; join with slip st to first dc:
168 dc.

Rnd 8: Ch 3, dc in next 12 dc, 2 dc in
next dc, (dc in next 13 dc, 2 dc in next dc)
around; join with slip st to first dc:
180 dc.

Continued on page 56.

Rnd 9: Ch 3, dc in next 6 dc, 2 dc in next dc, (dc in next 14 dc, 2 dc in next dc) around to last 7 dc, dc in last 7 dc; join with slip st to first dc: 192 dc.

Rnd 10: Ch 3, dc in same st and in next in next 15 dc, (2 dc in next dc, dc in next 15 dc) around; join with slip st to first dc: 204 dc.

Rnd 11: Ch 3, dc in next 15 dc, 2 dc in next dc, (dc in next 16 dc, 2 dc in next dc) around; join with slip st to first dc: 216 dc.

Rnd 12: Ch 3, dc in next 8 dc, 2 dc in next dc, (dc in next 17 dc, 2 dc in next dc) around to last 8 dc, dc in last 8 dc; join with slip st to first dc: 228 dc.

Rnd 13: Ch 3, dc in same st and in next in next 18 dc, (2 dc in next dc, dc in next 18 dc) around; join with slip st to first dc, finish off: 240 dc.

FIRST LEAF

Row 1: With **right** side facing, join Green with sc in any dc (**see Joining With Sc, page 92**); sc in next 24 dc, leave remaining 215 dc unworked: 25 sc.

Rows 2-13: Ch 1, turn; sc in each sc across.

Row 14: Ch 1, turn; work beginning decrease, sc in each sc across to last 2 sc, work ending decrease: 23 sc.

Row 15: Ch 1, turn; sc in each sc across.

Rows 16-22: Repeat Rows 14 and 15, 3 times; then repeat Row 14 once **more**: 15 sc.

Row 23: Ch 1, turn; skip first sc, sc in next 2 sc, hdc in next sc, dc in next 7 sc, hdc in next sc, sc in next 2 sc, slip st in last sc; finish off.

SECOND LEAF

Row 1: With **right** side facing, skip next 25 dc from First Leaf and join Green with sc in next dc; sc in next 24 dc, leave remaining 165 dc unworked: 25 sc.

Rows 2-23: Work same as First Leaf.

THIRD LEAF

Row 1: With **right** side facing, skip next 70 dc from Second Leaf and join Green with sc in next dc, sc in next 24 dc, leave remaining 70 dc unworked: 25 sc.

Rows 2-23: Work same as First Leaf.

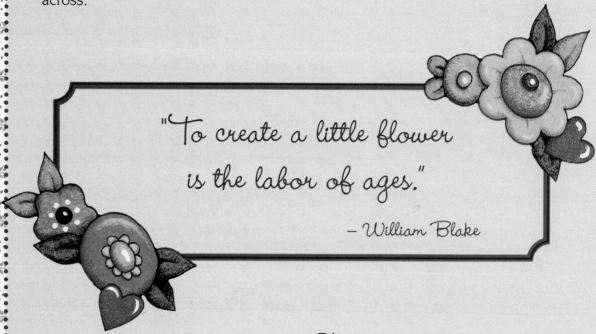

"To create a little flower is the labor of ages."

– William Blake

Bedroom Whimsies

For a fanciful transformation, just add a heaping helping of cherries and cream (in the form of this crocheted afghan and pillow set!) to a basic bedroom or guest room. Black and cream edging creates a hint of nostalgia, while charming cherries are delicious adornments in cross stitch. This stylish look is easy to master — just follow our charts to add the simple designs to rows of single crochet stitches. How sweet!

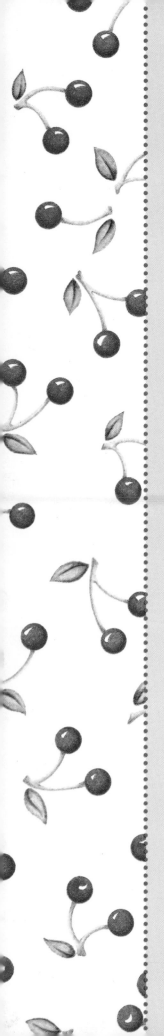

CROSS STITCH AFGHAN

Shown on page 59.

Finished Size: 48" x 64"
(122 cm x 162.5 cm)

MATERIALS
Worsted Weight Yarn:
Aran - 53 ounces, 2,995 yards
(1,510 grams, 2,738.5 meters)
Black - 1¹/₂ ounces, 85 yards
(40 grams, 77.5 meters)
Red - 40 yards (36.5 meters)
Green - 40 yards (36.5 meters)
Brown - 20 yards (18.5 meters)
Crochet hook, size H (5 mm) **or** size
needed for gauge
Yarn needle

GAUGE: 14 sc and 16 rows = 4" (10 cm)

Gauge Swatch: 4" (10 cm) square
Ch 15.
Work same as Afghan Body for 16 rows.
Finish off.

AFGHAN BODY

With Aran, ch 161 **loosely**.

Row 1 (Right side)**:** Sc in second ch from
hook and in each ch across: 160 sc.

Note: Loop a short piece of yarn around
any stitch to mark Row 1 as **right** side.

Rows 2-246: Ch 1, turn; sc in each sc
across; at end of Row 246, do **not**
finish off.

EDGING

Rnd 1: Ch 1, turn; 2 sc in first sc, sc in
each sc across to last sc, 2 sc in last sc;
working in end of rows, sc in same row
and in each row across; working in free
loops of beginning ch **(Fig. 3b, page 93),**
2 sc in first ch, sc in each ch across to ch
at base of last sc, 2 sc in ch at base of
last sc; sc in end of same row and in each
row across; join with slip st to first sc:
816 sc.

Rnd 2: Ch 1, do **not** turn; sc in same st,
ch 2, ★ sc in each sc across to second sc
of next corner 2-sc group, ch 2; repeat
from ★ 2 times **more**, sc in each sc
across; join with slip st to first sc: 816 sc
and 8 chs.

Rnd 3: (Slip st, ch 1, sc) in next ch, ch 8,
sc in next ch, drop loop from hook
leaving yarn to **right** side of work **(now
and throughout)** and working in **front** of
previous loop, join Black with sc in same
ch **(after** sc) as first Aran sc **(see Joining
With Sc, page 92)**; ch 8, sc in same ch as
next Aran sc **(after** sc), drop loop from
hook **(Fig. 1, page 61),** ★ † (slip hook in
first dropped loop, working in **front** of
previous loop, ch 8, sc in next unworked
sc, drop loop from hook) across to next
corner ch-2 †, [slip hook into first
dropped loop, working in **front** of
previous loop, ch 8, sc in next ch, drop
loop from hook, slip hook into first
dropped loop, working in **front** of
previous loop, ch 8, sc in same ch as last
sc made **(after** sc), drop loop from hook]
twice; repeat from ★ 2 times **more**, then
repeat from † to † once, slip hook into
first dropped loop, working in **front** of
previous loop, ch 8; join with slip st to
first sc of same color, finish off; slip hook
into last dropped loop, working in **front**
of previous loop, ch 8; working **behind**
first loop, join with slip st to first sc of
same color, finish off.

Fig. 1

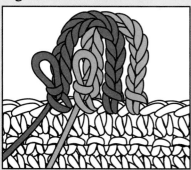

FINISHING

Follow Chart, page 95, for cross stitch design, randomly placing Cherries on Afghan.

SQUARE PILLOW

Shown on page 59.

Finished Size: 14" (35.5 cm) square

MATERIALS

Worsted Weight Yarn:
    Aran - 9$\frac{1}{2}$ ounces, 535 yards
      (270 grams, 489 meters)
    Black - 35 yards (32 meters)
    Red - 20 yards (18.5 meters)
    Green - 15 yards (13.5 meters)
    Brown - 10 yards (9 meters)
Crochet hook, size H (5 mm) **or** size
    needed for gauge
Square pillow form - 14" (35.5 cm) **or**
    2 - 14$\frac{1}{2}$" (37 cm) fabric squares,
    polyester fiberfill, and sewing
    needle and thread
Yarn needle

GAUGE: 14 sc and 16 rows = 4" (10 cm)

Gauge Swatch: 4" (10 cm) square
Ch 15.
Row 1: Sc in second ch from hook and in each ch across: 14 sc.
Rows 2-16: Ch 1, turn; sc in each sc across.
Finish off.

PILLOW FORM

With **right** sides together and using a $\frac{1}{4}$" (7 mm) seam, sew fabric squares together, leaving a 2" (5 cm) opening. Turn form right side out. Stuff firmly with polyester fiberfill and sew opening closed.

SIDE (Make 2)

With Aran, ch 48.

Row 1: Sc in second ch from hook and in each ch across: 47 sc.

Row 2 (Right side): Ch 1, turn; sc in each sc across.

Note: Loop a short piece of yarn around any stitch to mark Row 2 as **right** side and bottom edge.

Rows 3-54: Ch 1, turn; sc in each sc across.

Trim: Ch 1, do **not** turn; working in end of rows, sc in first row and in each row across; working in free loops of beginning ch **(Fig. 3b, page 93)**, 2 sc in ch at base of first sc and in each ch across to last ch, 2 sc in last ch; sc in same row and in each row across, 2 sc in next sc, sc in next sc and in each sc across to last sc, 2 sc in last sc; join with slip st to first sc, finish off: 206 sc.

61

Continued on page 62.

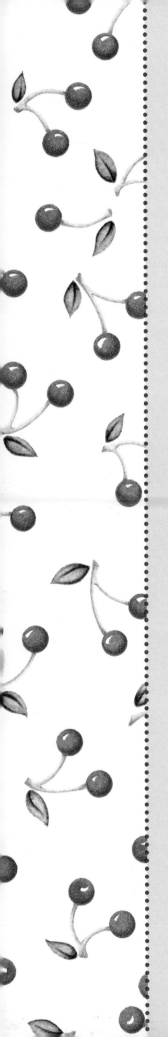

FINISHING

Follow chart, page 95, for cross stitch design, randomly placing Cherries on one Side.

EDGING

Rnd 1: With **wrong** sides and bottom edges of Sides together, cross stitch design facing you, and working through **both** thicknesses, join Aran with sc in first sc of any corner 2-sc group **(see Joining With Sc, page 92)**; ch 2, ★ sc in each sc across to second sc of next corner 2-sc group, ch 2; repeat from ★ 2 times **more**, sc in each sc across inserting pillow form before closing; join with slip st to first sc: 206 sc and 8 chs.

Rnd 2: Work same as Afghan Edging Rnd 3, page 60.

BOLSTER PILLOW

Shown on page 59.

Finished Size: 8" diameter x 18" length (20.5 cm x 45.5 cm)

MATERIALS

Worsted Weight Yarn:
  Aran - 10$^1/_2$ ounces, 595 yards (300 grams, 544 meters)
  Black - 35 yards (32 meters)
  Red - 20 yards (18.5 meters)
  Green - 15 yards (13.5 meters)
  Brown - 10 yards (9 meters)
Crochet hook, size H (5 mm) **or** size needed for gauge
Bolster pillow form - 8" x 18" (20.5 cm x 45.5 cm)
Yarn needle

GAUGE: 14 sc and 16 rows = 4" (10 cm); Rnds 1-3 of End = 2" (5 cm)

Gauge Swatch: 4" (10 cm) square
Ch 15.
Work same as Body, page 63, for 16 rows. Finish off.

END (Make 2)

Rnd 1 (Right side): With Aran, ch 2, 6 sc in second ch from hook; join with slip st to first sc.

Note: Loop a short piece of yarn around any stitch on Rnd 1 to mark **right** side.

Rnd 2: Ch 1, 2 sc in same st and in each sc around; join with slip st to first sc: 12 sc.

Rnd 3: Ch 1, 2 sc in same st, sc in next sc, (2 sc in next sc, sc in next sc) around; join with slip st to first sc: 18 sc.

Rnd 4: Ch 1, sc in same st and in next sc, 2 sc in next sc, (sc in next 2 sc, 2 sc in next sc) around; join with slip st to first sc: 24 sc.

Rnd 5: Ch 1, 2 sc in same st, sc in next 3 sc, (2 sc in next sc, sc in next 3 sc) around; join with slip st to first sc: 30 sc.

Rnd 6: Ch 1, sc in same st and in next 3 sc, 2 sc in next sc, (sc in next 4 sc, 2 sc in next sc) around; join with slip st to first sc: 36 sc.

Rnd 7: Ch 1, 2 sc in same st, sc in next 5 sc, (2 sc in next sc, sc in next 5 sc) around; join with slip st to first sc: 42 sc.

Rnd 8: Ch 1, sc in same st and in next 5 sc, 2 sc in next sc, (sc in next 6 sc, 2 sc in next sc) around; join with slip st to first sc: 48 sc.

Rnd 9: Ch 1, 2 sc in same st, sc in next 7 sc, (2 sc in next sc, sc in next 7 sc) around; join with slip st to first sc: 54 sc.

Rnd 10: Ch 1, sc in same st and in next 7 sc, 2 sc in next sc, (sc in next 8 sc, 2 sc in next sc) around; join with slip st to first sc: 60 sc.

Rnd 11: Ch 1, 2 sc in same st, sc in next 9 sc, (2 sc in next sc, sc in next 9 sc) around; join with slip st to first sc: 66 sc.

Rnd 12: Ch 1, sc in same st and in next 9 sc, 2 sc in next sc, (sc in next 10 sc, 2 sc in next sc) around; join with slip st to first sc: 72 sc.

Rnd 13: Ch 1, 2 sc in same st, sc in next 11 sc, (2 sc in next sc, sc in next 11 sc) around; join with slip st to first sc: 78 sc.

Rnd 14: Ch 1, sc in same st and in next 11 sc, 2 sc in next sc, (sc in next 12 sc, 2 sc in next sc) around; join with slip st to first sc: 84 sc.

Rnd 15: Ch 1, 2 sc in same st, sc in next 13 sc, (2 sc in next sc, sc in next 13 sc) around; join with slip st to first sc: 90 sc.

Rnd 16: Ch 1, sc in same st and in next 13 sc, 2 sc in next sc, (sc in next 14 sc, 2 sc in next sc) around; join with slip st to first sc: 96 sc.

Rnd 17: Ch 1, 2 sc in same st, sc in next 15 sc, (2 sc in next sc, sc in next 15 sc) around; join with slip st to first sc, finish off: 102 sc.

BODY

With Aran and leaving a long end for sewing, ch 62.

Row 1 (Right side): Sc in second ch from hook and in each ch across: 61 sc.

Note: Mark Row 1 as **right** side.

Rows 2-100: Ch 1, turn; sc in each sc across.

Finish off, leaving a long end for sewing.

FINISHING

Follow chart, page 95, for cross stitch design, randomly placing Cherries on Body.

With **right** side facing, sew last row to free loops of beginning ch **(Fig. 3b, page 93)**, leaving an opening in center for inserting pillow form.

Trim: With **right** side facing and working in end of rows, join Aran with sc in seam **(see Joining With Sc, page 92)**; work 101 sc evenly spaced around; join with slip st to first sc, finish off: 102 sc.

Repeat for opposite end.

JOINING

Rnd 1: With **wrong** sides of End and Body Trim together, working through **both** thicknesses, and with Body facing you, join Aran with sc in any sc; sc in next sc and in each sc around; join with slip st to first sc: 102 sc.

Rnd 2: Ch 1, sc in same st, ch 8, skip next sc, sc in next sc, drop loop from hook leaving yarn to **right** side of work **(now and throughout)**, working in **front** of Aran loop, join Black with sc in skipped sc; ch 8, sc in next unworked sc, drop loop from hook **(Fig. 1, page 61)**, ★ slip hook into first dropped loop, working in **front** of previous loop, ch 8, sc in next unworked sc, drop loop from hook; repeat from ★ around, slip hook into first dropped loop, working in **front** of previous loop, ch 8; join with slip st to first sc of same color, finish off; slip hook in last dropped loop, working in **front** of previous loop, ch 8; working **behind** first loop; join with slip st to first sc of same color, finish off.

Repeat for opposite End.

Insert pillow form and sew opening closed.

Fluff 'n' Stuff

Introduce a bit more fun into your daily routine with witty novelties to crochet. Sporting playful polka dots, a sweet Scottie dog toy and matching child's pullover make a precious combination. Pretty purses garnished with charming cherries are just right for a trip about town. And you'll simply adore our winsome teapot pincushion!

CHILD'S PULLOVER

Shown on page 65.

Size:	4	6	8	10
Finished Chest				
Measurement:	27"	29"	31"	32"
	68.5	73.5	78.5	81.5 cm

Size Note: Instructions are written for size 4 with sizes 6, 8 and 10 in braces { }. Instructions will be easier to read if you circle all the numbers pertaining to your size. If only one number is given, it applies to all sizes.

MATERIALS

Sport Weight Yarn:
  Red
    Ounces 13{14^1/$_2$-16^1/$_2$-18^1/$_2$}
    Yards 1,320{1,475-1,680-1,880}
    Grams 370{410-470-530}
    Meters 1,207{1,348.5-1,536-1,719}
  White - 50 yards (45.5 meters)
Crochet hooks, sizes F (3.75 mm) **and**
  G (4 mm) **or** sizes needed for gauge
Tapestry needle

GAUGE: 20 sc and 24 rows = 4" (10 cm)

Gauge Swatch: 4" (10 cm) square
With Red and larger size hook, ch 21.
Row 1: Sc in second ch from hook and in each ch across: 20 sc.
Rows 2-24: Ch 1, turn; sc in each sc across.
Finish off.

STITCH GUIDE

POPCORN
3 Sc in sc indicated changing to Red in last sc made (**Fig. 5, *page* 94**), drop loop from hook, insert hook in first sc of 3-sc group, hook dropped loop and draw through st.

BEGINNING DECREASE
  (uses first 2 sts)
Pull up a loop in first 2 sts, YO and draw through all 3 loops on hook (**counts as one sc**).

DECREASE (uses next 2 sts)
Pull up a loop in next 2 sts, YO and draw through all 3 loops on hook (**counts as one sc**).

BACK
RIBBING
With Red and using smaller size hook, ch 13.

Row 1: Sc in back ridge of second ch from hook (**Fig. 1, *page* 93**) and in each ch across: 12 sc.

Row 2: Ch 1, turn; sc in Back Loop Only of each sc across (**Fig. 2, *page* 93**).

Repeat Row 2 until 34{37-39-40} ribs [68{74-78-80} rows] are complete; do **not** finish off.

BODY

Change to larger size hook.

Row 1 (Right side): Ch 1, do **not** turn; sc in end of each row across: 68{74-78-80} sc.

Note: Loop a short piece of yarn around any stitch to mark Row 1 as **right** side.

Rows 2-4: Ch 1, turn; sc in each sc across.

Row 5: Ch 1, turn; working over White with Red, sc in first 10{12-6-7} sc changing to White in last sc made **(Fig. 5, page 94)**, work Popcorn in next sc, ★ sc in next 15 sc changing to White in last sc made, work Popcorn in next sc; repeat from ★ 2{2-3-3} times **more**, working over White, with Red sc in each sc across; cut White: 64{70-73-75} sc and 4{4-5-5} Popcorns.

Continue changing colors in same manner throughout.

Rows 6-16: Ch 1, turn; sc in each st across.

Row 17: Ch 1, turn; working over White, with Red sc in first 2{5-14-15} sc, with White work Popcorn in next sc, ★ with Red sc in next 15 sc, with White work Popcorn in next sc; repeat from ★ 2{3-2-2} times **more**, working over White, with Red sc in each sc across; cut White: 64{69-74-76} sc and 4{5-4-4} Popcorns.

Rows 18-28: Ch 1, turn; sc in each st across.

Repeat Rows 5-28 for pattern until Back measures approximately 14$^1/_2${16-17$^1/_2$-19}" /37{40.5-44.5-48.5} cm from bottom edge, ending by working a **right** side row; do **not** finish off.

LEFT NECK SHAPING

Maintain established pattern throughout.

Row 1: Ch 1, turn; work across first 25{28-28-29} sts, leave remaining sts unworked: 25{28-28-29} sts.

Row 2 (Decrease row): Ch 1, turn; work beginning decrease, work across: 24{27-27-28} sts.

Row 3 (Decrease row): Ch 1, turn; work across to last 2 sts, decrease: 23{26-26-27} sts.

Rows 4-6: Repeat Rows 2 and 3 once, then repeat Row 3 once **more**; finish off leaving a long end for sewing: 20{23-23-24} sts.

RIGHT NECK SHAPING

Maintain established pattern throughout.

Row 1: With **wrong** side facing, skip 18{18-22-22} sts from Left Neck and join Red with sc in next st **(see Joining With Sc, page 92)**; work across: 25{28-28-29} sts.

Row 2 (Decrease row): Ch 1, turn; work across to last 2 sts, decrease: 24{27-27-28} sts.

Row 3 (Decrease row): Ch 1, turn; work beginning decrease, work across: 23{26-26-27} sts.

Rows 4-6: Repeat Rows 2 and 3 once, then repeat Row 3 once **more**; finish off leaving a long end for sewing: 20{23-23-24} sts.

Continued on page 68.

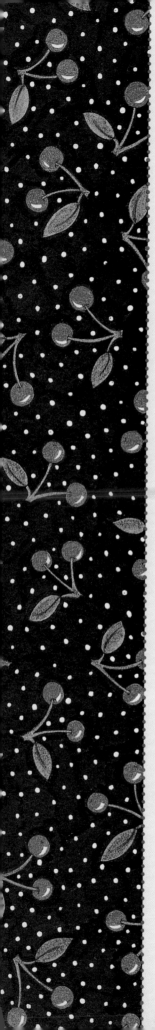

FRONT

Work same as Back until Front measures approximately 13½{14¾-16¼-17½}" /34.5{37.5-41.5-44.5} cm from bottom edge, ending by working a **right** side row; do **not** finish off.

RIGHT NECK SHAPING

Maintain established pattern throughout.

Row 1: Ch 1, turn; work across first 25{28-28-29} sts, leave remaining sts unworked: 25{28-28-29} sts.

Row 2: Ch 1, turn; work beginning decrease, work across: 24{27-27-28} sts.

Row 3: Ch 1, turn; work across to last 2 sts, decrease: 23{26-26-27} sts.

Row 4 (Decrease row): Ch 1, turn; work beginning decrease, work across: 22{25-25-26} sts.

Row 5: Ch 1, turn; work across.

Rows 6-9: Repeat Rows 4 and 5 twice: 20{23-23-24} sts.

Work even until Right Neck measures same as Back, ending by working a **right** side row; finish off.

LEFT NECK SHAPING

Maintain established pattern throughout.

Row 1: With **wrong** side facing, skip 18{18-22-22} sts from Right Neck and join Red with sc in next st; work across: 25{28-28-29} sts.

Row 2: Ch 1, turn; work across to last 2 sts, decrease: 24{27-27-28} sts.

Row 3: Ch 1, turn; work beginning decrease, work across: 23{26-26-27} sts.

Row 4 (Decrease row): Ch 1, turn; work across to last 2 sts, decrease: 22{25-25-26} sts.

Row 5: Ch 1, turn; work across.

Rows 6-9: Repeat Rows 4 and 5 twice: 20{23-23-24} sts.

Work even until Left Neck measures same as Back, ending by working a **right** side row; finish off.

SLEEVE (Make 2)
RIBBING

With Red and using smaller size hook, ch 15.

Row 1: Sc in back ridge of second ch from hook and in each ch across: 14 sc.

Row 2: Ch 1, turn; sc in Back Loop Only of each sc across.

Repeat Row 2 until 16{16-17-17} ribs [32{32-34-34} rows] are complete; do **not** finish off.

BODY

Change to larger size hook.

Row 1 (Right side): Ch 1, do **not** turn; sc in end of each row across: 32{32-34-34} sc.

Note: Mark Row 1 as **right** side.

Row 2: Ch 1, turn; 2 sc in first sc, sc in next sc and in each sc across to last sc, 2 sc in last sc: 34{34-36-36} sc.

Row 3: Ch 1, turn; sc in each sc across.

Row 4: Ch 1, turn; 2 sc in first sc, sc in next sc and in each sc across to last sc, 2 sc in last sc: 36{36-38-38} sc.

Row 5: Ch 1, turn; working over White, with Red sc in first 7{7-9-9} sc, with White work Popcorn in next sc, with Red sc in next 15 sc, with White work Popcorn in next sc, with Red sc in each sc across; cut White: 34{34-36-36} sc and 2 Popcorns.

Row 6: Ch 1, turn; 2 sc in first sc, sc in next st and in each st across to last sc, 2 sc in last sc: 38{38-40-40} sc.

Row 7: Ch 1, turn; sc in each sc across.

SIZE 4 ONLY
Rows 8 and 9: Ch 1, turn; sc in each sc across.

Row 10 (Increase row)**:** Ch 1, turn; 2 sc in first sc, sc in next sc and in each st across to last sc, 2 sc in last sc: 40 sc.

Rows 11-16: Repeat Rows 7-10 once, then repeat Rows 7 and 8 once **more**: 42 sc.

Row 17: Ch 1, turn; working over White, with Red sc in first 2 sc, with White work Popcorn in next sc, ★ with Red sc in next 15 sc, with White work Popcorn in next sc; repeat from ★ once **more**, working over White, with Red sc in each sc across; cut White: 39 sc and 3 Popcorns.

Row 18: Repeat Row 10: 44 sc.

Rows 19-28: Repeat Rows 7-10 twice, then repeat Rows 7 and 8 once **more**: 48 sc.

Row 29: Ch 1, turn; working over White, with Red sc in first 13 sc, with White work Popcorn in next sc, ★ with Red sc in next 15 sc, with White work Popcorn in next sc; repeat from ★ once **more**, working over White, with Red sc in each sc across; cut White: 45 sc and 3 Popcorns.

Row 30: Repeat Row 10: 50 sc.

Rows 31-40: Repeat Rows 7-10 twice, then repeat Rows 7 and 8 once **more**: 54 sc.

Row 41: Ch 1, turn; working over White, with Red sc in first 8 sc, with White work Popcorn in next sc, ★ with Red sc in next 15 sc, with White work Popcorn in next sc; repeat from ★ once **more**, working over White, with Red sc in each sc across; cut White: 51 sc and 3 Popcorns.

Row 42: Repeat Row 10: 56 sc.

Rows 43-50: Repeat Rows 7-10 twice; at end of Row 50, finish off: 60 sc.

SIZE 6 ONLY
Row 8 (Increase row)**:** Ch 1, turn; 2 sc in first sc, sc in next sc and in each st across to last sc, 2 sc in last sc: 40 sc.

Rows 9-11: Ch 1, turn; sc in each st across.

Rows 12-16: Repeat Rows 8-11 once, then repeat Row 8 once **more**: 44 sc.

Row 17: Ch 1, turn; working over White, with Red sc in first 3 sc, with White work Popcorn in next sc, ★ with Red sc in next 15 sc, with White work Popcorn in next sc; repeat from ★ once **more**, working over White, with Red sc in each sc across; cut White: 41 sc and 3 Popcorns.

Rows 18 and 19: Ch 1, turn; sc in each st across.

Rows 20-28: Repeat Rows 8-11 twice, then repeat Row 8 once **more**: 50 sc.

Row 29: Ch 1, turn; working over White, with Red sc in first 14 sc, with White work Popcorn in next sc, ★ with Red sc in next 15 sc, with White work Popcorn in next sc; repeat from ★ once **more**, working over White, with Red sc in each sc across; cut White: 47 sc and 3 Popcorns.

Rows 30 and 31: Ch 1, turn; sc in each st across.

Continued on page 70.

Rows 32-40: Repeat Rows 8-11 twice, then repeat Row 8 once **more**: 56 sc.

Row 41: Ch 1, turn; working over White, with Red sc in first 9 sc, with White work Popcorn in next sc, ★ with Red sc in next 15 sc, with White work Popcorn in next sc; repeat from ★ once **more**, working over White, with Red sc in each sc across; cut White: 53 sc and 3 Popcorns.

Rows 42 and 43: Ch 1, turn; sc in each st across.

Rows 44-52: Repeat Rows 8-11 twice, then repeat Row 8 once **more**: 62 sc.

Row 53: Ch 1, turn; working over White, with Red sc in first 4 sc, with White work Popcorn in next sc, ★ with Red sc in next 15 sc, with White work Popcorn in next sc; repeat from ★ 2 times **more**, working over White, with Red sc in each sc across; cut White: 58 sc and 4 Popcorns.

Rows 54 and 55: Ch 1, turn; sc in each st across.

Row 56: Repeat Row 8; finish off: 64 sc.

SIZES 8 AND 10 ONLY
Row 8 (Increase row)**:** Ch 1, turn; 2 sc in first sc, sc in next sc and in each st across to last sc, 2 sc in last sc: 42 sc.

Row 9: Ch 1, turn; sc in each st across.

Rows 10-14: Repeat Rows 8 and 9 twice, then repeat Row 8 once **more**: 48 sc.

Rows 15 and 16: Ch 1, turn; sc in each st across.

Row 17: Ch 1, turn; working over White, with Red sc in first {6-6} sc, with White work Popcorn in next sc, ★ with Red sc in next 15 sc, with White work Popcorn in next sc; repeat from ★ once **more**, working over White, with Red sc in each sc across; cut White: {45-45} sc and 3 Popcorns.

Row 18 (Increase Row)**:** Ch 1, turn; 2 sc in first sc, sc in next sc and in each st across to last sc, 2 sc in last sc: {50-50} sc.

Rows 19-21: Ch 1, turn; sc in each st across.

Rows 22-28: Repeat Rows 18-21 once, then repeat Rows 18-20 once **more**: {54-54} sc.

Row 29: Ch 1, turn; working over White, with Red sc in first {17-17} sc, with White work Popcorn in next sc, ★ with Red sc in next 15 sc, with White work Popcorn in next sc; repeat from ★ once **more**, working over White, with Red sc in each sc across; cut White: {51-51} sc and 3 Popcorns.

Rows 30-40: Repeat Rows 18-21 twice, then repeat Rows 18-20 once **more**: {60-60} sc.

Row 41: Ch 1, turn; working over White, with Red sc in first {12-12} sc, with White work Popcorn in next sc, ★ with Red sc in next 15 sc, with White work Popcorn in next sc; repeat from ★ once **more**, working over White, with Red sc in each sc across; cut White: {57-57} sc and 3 Popcorns.

Rows 42-52: Repeat Rows 18-21 twice, then repeat Rows 18-20 once **more**: {66-66} sc.

Row 53: Ch 1, turn; working over White, with Red sc in first {7-7} sc, with White work Popcorn in next sc, ★ with Red sc in next 15 sc, with White work Popcorn in next sc; repeat from ★ 2 times **more**, working over White, with Red sc in each sc across; cut White: {62-62} sc and 4 Popcorns.

SIZE 8 ONLY

Rows 54-60: Repeat Rows 18-21 once, then repeat Rows 18-20 once **more**: 70 sts.

Finish off.

SIZE 10 ONLY

Rows 54-64: Repeat Rows 18-21 twice, then repeat Rows 18-20 once **more**: 72 sc.

Row 65: Ch 1, turn; working over White, with Red sc in first 18 sc, with White work Popcorn in next sc, ★ with Red sc in next 15 sc, with White work Popcorn in next sc; repeat from ★ 2 times **more**, working over White, with Red sc in each sc across; cut White: 68 sc and 4 Popcorns.

Rows 66-68: Repeat Rows 18-20: 74 sc.

Finish off.

FINISHING

Sew shoulder seams.

NECKBAND

Foundation Rnd: With **right** side facing and using smaller size hook, join Red with sc in right shoulder seam; work 6 sc evenly spaced along Right Back Neck edge, sc in each sc across Back, work 6 sc evenly spaced across Left Back Neck edge, sc in left shoulder seam, work 12{13-13-15} sc evenly spaced along Left Front Neck edge, sc in each sc across Front, work 12{13-13-15} sc evenly spaced along Right Front Neck edge; join with slip st to first sc: 74{76-84-88} sc.

Ch 13.

Row 1: Sc in back ridge of second ch from hook and in each ch across, sc in first 2 sc on Foundation Rnd: 14 sc.

Row 2: Turn; skip first 2 sc, sc in Back Loop Only of each sc across: 12 sc.

Row 3: Ch 1, turn; sc in Back Loop Only of next 12 sc, sc in **both** loops of next 2 sc on Foundation Rnd: 14 sc.

Repeat Rows 2 and 3 around, ending by working Row 2.

Last Row: Ch 1, turn; sc in Back Loop Only of next 12 sc, slip st in **both** loops of last sc on Foundation Rnd; finish off leaving a long end for sewing.

Sew seam.

Sew Sleeves to Pullover, matching center of last row on Sleeve to shoulder seam and beginning 6{6½-7-7½}"/15{16.5-18-19} cm down from seam.

Weave underarm and side in one continuous seam (**Fig. 1**).

WEAVING SEAMS

With the **right** side of both pieces facing you and edges even, sew through both sides once to secure the seam, leaving an ample yarn end to weave in later. Insert the needle from **right** to **left** through two strands on each piece (**Fig. 1**). Bring the needle around and insert it from **right** to **left** on **both** pieces. Continue in this manner, drawing the seam together as you work.

Fig. 1

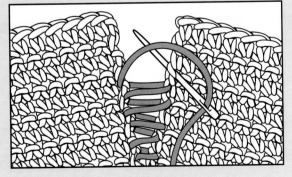

SCOTTIE DOG TOY

Shown on page 65.

Finished Size: 14"h x 21"l
(35.5 cm x 53.5 cm)

MATERIALS
Worsted Weight Yarn,
11½ ounces, 650 yards
(330 grams, 594.5 meters)
Crochet hook, size G (4 mm) **or** size
needed for gauge
¾" (19 mm) White two-hole button - 2
⁹⁄₁₆" (14 mm) Black two-hole button - 2
Polyester fiberfill
Yarn needle

GAUGE: 16 sc and 18 rows = 4" (10 cm)

Gauge Swatch: 4" (10 cm) square
Ch 17.
Row 1: Sc in second ch from hook and in each ch across: 16 sc.
Rows 2-18: Ch 1, turn; sc in each sc across.
Finish off.

STITCH GUIDE

> **JOINING DECREASE**
> Begin with a slip knot on hook. Pull up a loop in each sc indicated, YO and draw through all 3 loops on hook **(counts as one sc)**.
>
> **BEGINNING DECREASE**
> Pull up a loop in first 2 sc, YO and draw through all 3 loops on hook **(counts as one sc)**.
>
> **DECREASE**
> Pull up a loop in next 2 sc, YO and draw through all 3 loops on hook **(counts as one sc)**.

> **3-SC DECREASE**
> Pull up a loop in next 3 sc, YO and draw through all 4 loops on hook **(counts as one sc)**.
>
> **ENDING DECREASE**
> Pull up a loop in last 2 sc, YO and draw through all 3 loops on hook **(counts as one sc)**.
>
> **FRONT POST SINGLE CROCHET (***abbreviated* FP*sc***)**
> Insert hook from **front** to **back** around post of next sc **(Fig. 4, page 93)**, YO and pull up a loop, YO and draw through both loops on hook. Skip st behind FPsc.

Make pieces in order written, setting them aside until needed for joining or finishing.

EAR (Make 2)
Ch 10, leaving a long end for sewing.

Rnd 1 (Right side)**:** Sc in second ch from hook and in each ch across; working in free loops of beginning ch **(Fig. 3b, page 93)**, sc in each ch across; join with slip st to first sc: 18 sc.

Note: Loop a short piece of yarn around any sc to mark Rnd 1 as **right** side.

Rnd 2: Ch 1, turn; 2 sc in first sc, sc in next 7 sc, 2 sc in each of next 2 sc, sc in next 7 sc, 2 sc in last sc; join with slip st to first sc: 22 sc.

Rnds 3-10: Ch 1, turn; sc in each sc around; join with slip st to first sc.

Rnd 11: Ch 1, turn; work beginning decrease, sc in next 9 sc, decrease, sc in last 9 sc; join with slip st to first sc: 20 sc.

Rnd 12: Ch 1, turn; work beginning decrease, sc in next 8 sc, decrease, sc in last 8 sc; join with slip st to first sc: 18 sc.

Rnd 13: Ch 1, turn; work beginning decrease, sc in next 7 sc, decrease, sc in last 7 sc; join with slip st to first sc: 16 sc.

Rnd 14: Ch 1, turn; work beginning decrease, sc in next 6 sc, decrease, sc in last 6 sc; join with slip st to first sc: 14 sc.

Rnd 15: Ch 1, turn; work beginning decrease, sc in next 5 sc, decrease, sc in last 5 sc; join with slip st to first sc: 12 sc.

Rnd 16: Ch 1, turn; work beginning decrease, sc in next 2 sc, decrease twice, sc in next 2 sc, work ending decrease; join with slip st to first sc: 8 sc.

Rnd 17: Ch 1, turn; decrease around; join with slip st to first sc; finish off leaving a long end for weaving.

Thread needle with long end, weave through tops of stitches on Rnd 17; gather tightly to close and secure end.

SOLES OF FEET
BACK FOOT (Make 2)
Rnd 1 (Right side): Ch 2, 6 sc in second ch from hook; join with slip st to first sc.

Note: Mark Rnd 1 as **right** side and piece as Sole of Back Foot.

Rnd 2: Ch 1, turn; 2 sc in each sc around; join with slip st to first sc: 12 sc.

Rnd 3: Ch 1, turn; sc in first 2 sc, 2 sc in each of next 2 sc, (sc in next 2 sc, 2 sc in each of next 2 sc) around; join with slip st to first sc: 18 sc.

Rnd 4: Ch 1, turn; sc in first 4 sc, 2 sc in each of next 2 sc, (sc in next 4 sc, 2 sc in each of next 2 sc) around; join with slip st to first sc: 24 sc.

Rnd 5: Ch 1, turn; sc in first 3 sc, 2 sc in next sc, (sc in next 3 sc, 2 sc in next sc) around; join with slip st to first sc: 30 sc.

Rnd 6: Ch 1, turn; sc in first 3 sc, 2 sc in next sc, (sc in next 3 sc, 2 sc in next sc) 5 times, (sc in next 2 sc, 2 sc in next sc) twice; join with slip st to first sc, finish off: 38 sc.

FRONT FOOT (Make 2)
Rnd 1 (Right side): Ch 2, 6 sc in second ch from hook; join with slip st to first sc.

Note: With contrasting color yarn, mark Rnd 1 as **right** side and piece as Sole of Front Foot.

Rnd 2: Ch 1, turn; 2 sc in each sc around; join with slip st to first sc: 12 sc.

Rnd 3: Ch 1, turn; sc in first 2 sc, 2 sc in each of next 2 sc, (sc in next 2 sc, 2 sc in each of next 2 sc) around; join with slip st to first sc: 18 sc.

Rnd 4: Ch 1, turn; sc in first 4 sc, 2 sc in each of next 2 sc, (sc in next 4 sc, 2 sc in each of next 2 sc) around; join with slip st to first sc: 24 sc.

Rnd 5: Ch 1, turn; sc in first 5 sc, 2 sc in next sc, (sc in next 5 sc, 2 sc in next sc) around; join with slip st to first sc: 28 sc.

Rnd 6: Ch 1, turn; sc in first 4 sc, 2 sc in next sc, (sc in next 4 sc, 2 sc in next sc) 4 times, sc in last 3 sc; join with slip st to first sc; finish off: 33 sc.

TOP
TAIL
Row 1 (Right side): Ch 2, 5 sc in second ch from hook.

Note: Mark Row 1 as **right** side.

Row 2: Ch 1, turn; 2 sc in each across: 10 sc.

Continued on page 74.

Row 3: Ch 1, turn; 2 sc in each of first 2 sc, sc in next 6 sc, 2 sc in each of last 2 sc: 14 sc.

Row 4: Ch 1, turn; 2 sc in first sc, sc in next sc and in each sc across to last sc, 2 sc in last sc: 16 sc.

Rows 5-15: Ch 1, turn; sc in each sc across.

Finish off.

BACK OF FIRST LEG
Ch 28.

Row 1 (Right side): Working in back ridge of chs **(Fig. 1, *page 93*)**, 2 sc in second ch from hook, sc in next ch and in each ch across: 28 sc.

Note: Mark Row 1 as **right** side.

Row 2: Ch 1, turn; sc in each sc across to last sc, 2 sc in last sc: 29 sc.

Row 3: Ch 1, turn; 2 sc in first sc, sc in next sc and in each sc across: 30 sc.

Row 4: Ch 1, turn; sc in each sc across to last sc, 2 sc in last sc; finish off: 31 sc.

BACK OF SECOND LEG
Ch 28.

Row 1 (Right side): Working in back ridge of chs, sc in second ch from hook and in each ch across to last ch, 2 sc in last ch: 28 sc.

Note: Mark Row 1 as **right** side.

Row 2: Ch 1, turn; 2 sc in first sc, sc in next sc and in each sc across: 29 sc.

Row 3: Ch 1, turn; sc in each sc across to last sc, 2 sc in last sc: 30 sc.

Row 4: Ch 1, turn; 2 sc in first sc, sc in next sc and in each sc across; do **not** finish off: 31 sc.

BACK LEGS

Row 1 (Joining Row): Ch 1, turn; sc in each sc across; with **right** side of Tail facing, skip first 2 sc, sc in next 12 sc, leave last 2 sc unworked, with **right** side of Back of First Leg facing, sc in first sc and in each sc across: 74 sc.

Rows 2-13: Ch 1, turn; sc in each sc across.

Do **not** finish off.

FRONT OF FIRST LEG

Row 1: Ch 1, turn; sc in first 8 sc, decrease, leave remaining 64 sc on Back Legs unworked: 9 sc.

Row 2: Ch 1, turn; work beginning decrease, sc in each sc across: 8 sc.

Row 3: Ch 1, turn; sc in first 6 sc, work ending decrease; finish off: 7 sc.

FRONT OF SECOND LEG

Row 1: With **wrong** side of Back Legs facing, skip next 54 unworked sc and work joining decrease in next 2 sc; sc in last 8 sc: 9 sc.

Row 2: Ch 1, turn; sc in first 7 sc, work ending decrease: 8 sc.

Row 3: Ch 1, turn; work beginning decrease, sc in last 6 sc; finish off: 7 sc.

BODY

Row 1: With **wrong** side of Back Legs facing, working in 54 unworked sc, skip first 4 sc and join yarn with sc in next sc **(see Joining With Sc, *page 92*)**; sc in same st and in next 44 sc, 2 sc in next sc, leave remaining 4 sc unworked: 48 sc.

Rows 2-9: Ch 1, turn; 2 sc in first sc, sc in next sc and in each sc across to last sc, 2 sc in last sc: 64 sc.

Rows 10-19: Ch 1, turn; sc in each sc across.

Rows 20-27: Ch 1, turn; work beginning decrease, sc in next sc and in each sc across to last 2 sc, work ending decrease: 48 sc.

Finish off.

FRONT LEGS

Row 1: Ch 14, with **right** side of Body facing, work beginning decrease, sc in next sc and in each sc across to last 2 sc, work ending decrease, ch 15: 46 sc and 29 chs.

Row 2: Turn; sc in back ridge of second ch from hook and in next 13 chs, sc in next 46 sc, sc in back ridge of last 14 chs: 74 sc.

Row 3: Ch 1, turn; sc in each sc across.

Row 4: Ch 1, turn; sc in first 36 sc, 2 sc in each of next 2 sc, sc in last 36 sc: 76 sc.

Row 5: Ch 1, turn; sc in first 37 sc, 2 sc in each of next 2 sc, sc in last 37 sc: 78 sc.

Row 6: Ch 1, turn; sc in first 38 sc, 2 sc in each of next 2 sc, sc in last 38 sc: 80 sc.

Row 7: Ch 1, turn; sc in first 39 sc, 2 sc in each of next 2 sc, sc in last 39 sc: 82 sc.

Row 8: Ch 1, turn; sc in first 40 sc, 2 sc in each of next 2 sc, sc in last 40 sc: 84 sc.

Row 9: Ch 1, turn; sc in first 41 sc, 2 sc in each of next 2 sc, sc in last 41 sc: 86 sc.

Row 10: Ch 1, turn; sc in first 42 sc, 2 sc in each of next 2 sc, sc in last 42 sc: 88 sc.

Row 11: Ch 1, turn; sc in first 43 sc, 2 sc in each of next 2 sc, sc in last 43 sc: 90 sc.

Row 12: Ch 1, turn; sc in first 44 sc, 2 sc in each of next 2 sc, sc in last 44 sc: 92 sc.

Row 13: Ch 1, turn; sc in first 45 sc, 2 sc in each of next 2 sc, sc in last 45 sc; do **not** finish off: 94 sc.

FRONT OF THIRD LEG

Row 1: Ch 1, turn; sc in first 8 sc, decrease, leave remaining 84 sc unworked: 9 sc.

Row 2: Ch 1, turn; work beginning decrease, sc in last 7 sc: 8 sc.

Row 3: Ch 1, turn; sc in first 6 sc, work ending decrease; finish off: 7 sc.

FRONT OF LAST LEG

Row 1: With **wrong** side of Front Legs facing, skip next 74 unworked sc and work joining decrease in next 2 sc; sc in last 8 sc: 9 sc.

Row 2: Ch 1, turn; sc in first 7 sc, work ending decrease: 8 sc.

Row 3: Ch 1, turn; work beginning decrease, sc in last 6 sc; finish off: 7 sc.

HEAD

Row 1: With **wrong** side of Front Legs facing and working in 74 unworked sc, skip first 8 sc and work joining decrease in next 2 sc, sc in next 26 sc, 2 sc in each of next 2 sc, sc in next 26 sc, decrease, leave remaining 8 sc unworked: 58 sc.

Rows 2 and 3: Ch 1, turn; work beginning decrease, sc in next 26 sc, 2 sc in each of next 2 sc, sc in next 26 sc, work ending decrease.

Rows 4 and 5: Ch 1, turn; sc in each sc across.

Rows 6 and 7: Ch 1, turn; 2 sc in first sc, sc in next sc and in each sc across to last sc, 2 sc in last sc: 62 sc.

Continued on page 76.

Row 8: Ch 1, turn; sc in each sc across.

Row 9: Ch 1, turn; 2 sc in first sc, sc in next sc and in each sc across to last sc, 2 sc in last sc: 64 sc.

Row 10: Ch 1, turn; sc in first 31 sc, 2 sc in next sc, sc in last 32 sc: 65 sc.

Rows 11-13: Ch 1, turn; 2 sc in first sc, sc in next sc and in each sc across to last sc, 2 sc in last sc: 71 sc.

Row 14: Ch 1, turn; 2 sc in first sc, sc in next 21 sc, decrease, sc in next 23 sc, decrease, sc in next sc and in each sc across to last sc, 2 sc in last sc.

Row 15: Ch 1, turn; 2 sc in first sc, sc in next 22 sc, decrease, sc in next 21 sc, decrease, sc in next sc and in each sc across to last sc, 2 sc in last sc.

Row 16: Ch 1, turn; 2 sc in first sc, sc in next 23 sc, decrease, sc in next 19 sc, decrease, sc in next sc and in each sc across to last sc, 2 sc in last sc.

Row 17: Ch 1, turn; 2 sc in first sc, sc in next 24 sc, decrease, sc in next 17 sc, decrease, sc in next sc and in each sc across to last sc, 2 sc in last sc.

Row 18: Ch 1, turn; 2 sc in first sc, sc in next 25 sc, decrease, sc in next 15 sc, decrease, sc in next sc and in each sc across to last sc, 2 sc in last sc.

Row 19: Ch 1, turn; 2 sc in first sc, sc in next 26 sc, decrease, sc in next 13 sc, decrease, sc in next sc and in each sc across to last sc, 2 sc in last sc.

Row 20: Ch 1, turn; work beginning decrease, sc in next 26 sc, decrease, sc in next 4 sc, work 3-sc decrease, sc in next 4 sc, decrease, sc in next sc and in each sc across to last 2 sc, work ending decrease: 65 sc.

Row 21: Ch 1, turn; work beginning decrease, sc in next 25 sc, decrease, sc in next 2 sc, work 3-sc decrease, sc in next 2 sc, decrease, sc in next sc and in each sc across to last 2 sc, work ending decrease: 59 sc.

Row 22: Ch 1, turn; work beginning decrease, sc in next 24 sc, decrease, sc in next 3 sc, decrease, sc in next sc and in each sc across to last 2 sc, work ending decrease: 55 sc.

Row 23: Ch 1, turn, work beginning decrease, sc in next sc and in each sc across to last 2 sc, work ending decrease: 53 sc.

Row 24: Ch 1, turn; work beginning decrease, sc in next 20 sc, work 3 FPsc, [(insert hook from **front** to **back** around post of next sc, YO and pull up a loop) 3 times, YO and draw through all 4 loops on hook **(counts as one sc)**], skip 3 sc behind sc just made, work 3 FPsc, sc in next sc and in each sc across to last 2 sc, work ending decrease: 49 sc.

Row 25: Ch 1, turn; work beginning decrease, sc in next 21 sc, work 3-sc decrease, sc in next sc and in each sc across to last 2 sc, work ending decrease: 45 sc.

Row 26: Ch 1, turn; work beginning decrease, sc in next 19 sc, work 3-sc decrease, sc in next sc and in each sc across to last 2 sc, work ending decrease: 41 sc.

Row 27: Ch 1, turn; work beginning decrease, sc in next 17 sc, work 3-sc decrease, sc in next sc and in each sc across to last 2 sc, work ending decrease: 37 sc.

Row 28: Ch 1, turn; work beginning decrease, sc in next 15 sc, work 3-sc decrease, sc in next sc and in each sc across to last 2 sc, work ending decrease: 33 sc.

Row 29: Ch 1, turn; work beginning decrease, sc in next 13 sc, work 3-sc decrease, sc in next sc and in each sc across to last 2 sc, work ending decrease: 29 sc.

Row 30: Ch 1, turn; work beginning decrease, sc in next 11 sc, work 3-sc decrease, sc in next sc and in each sc across to last 2 sc, work ending decrease: 25 sc.

Row 31: Ch 1, turn; work beginning decrease, sc in next 9 sc, work 3-sc decrease, sc in next sc and in each sc across to last 2 sc, work ending decrease: 21 sc.

Row 32: Ch 1, turn; work beginning decrease, sc in next 7 sc, work 3-sc decrease, sc in next sc and in each sc across to last 2 sc, work ending decrease: 17 sc.

Row 33: Ch 1, turn; work beginning decrease, sc in next 5 sc, work 3-sc decrease, sc in next sc and in each sc across to last 2 sc, work ending decrease: 13 sc.

Row 34: Ch 1, turn; work beginning decrease, sc in next 3 sc, work 3-sc decrease, sc in next sc and in each sc across to last 2 sc, work ending decrease: 9 sc.

Row 35: Ch 1, turn; work beginning decrease, sc in next sc, work 3-sc decrease, sc in next sc, work ending decrease: 5 sc.

Row 36: Ch 1, turn; sc in each sc across; finish off.

UNDERNEATH OF BODY
BOTTOM

Ch 5.

Row 1 (Right side): Sc in back ridge of second ch from hook and in each ch across: 4 sc.

Note: Mark Row 1 as **right** side.

Rows 2 and 3: Ch 1, turn; 2 sc in first sc, sc in next sc and in each sc across to last sc, 2 sc in last sc: 8 sc.

Rows 4-16: Ch 1, turn; sc in each sc across.

Finish off.

BACK LEGS

Row 1: Ch 14, with **right** side of Bottom facing, sc in each sc across, ch 15: 8 sc and 29 chs.

Row 2: Turn; sc in back ridge of second ch from hook and in next 13 chs, sc in next 8 sc, sc in back ridge of last 14 chs: 36 sc.

Rows 3-8: Ch 1, turn; sc in each sc across.

Row 9: Ch 1, turn; sc in first 14 sc, decrease, sc in next 4 sc, decrease, sc in last 14 sc: 34 sc.

Row 10: Ch 1, turn; sc in each sc across.

Row 11: Ch 1, turn; sc in first 14 sc, decrease, sc in next 2 sc, decrease, sc in last 14 sc: 32 sc.

Rows 12 and 13: Ch 1, turn; sc in each sc across.

Row 14: Ch 1, turn; sc in first 15 sc, 2 sc in each of next 2 sc, sc in last 15 sc; do **not** finish off: 34 sc.

Continued on page 78.

FRONT OF FIRST LEG

Row 1: Ch 1, turn; sc in first 8 sc, decrease, leave remaining 24 sc unworked: 9 sc.

Row 2: Ch 1, turn; work beginning decrease, sc in last 7 sc: 8 sc.

Row 3: Ch 1, turn; sc in first 6 sc, work ending decrease; finish off: 7 sc.

FRONT OF SECOND LEG

Row 1: With **right** side of Back Legs facing, skip next 14 unworked sc and work joining decrease in next 2 sc; sc in last 8 sc: 9 sc.

Row 2: Ch 1, turn; sc in first 7 sc, work ending decrease: 8 sc.

Row 3: Ch 1, turn; work beginning decrease, sc in last 6 sc; finish off: 7 sc.

BELLY

Row 1: With **right** side of Back Legs facing and working in 14 unworked sc, skip first 4 sc and join yarn with sc in next sc; sc in same st and in next 4 sc, 2 sc in next sc, leave remaining 4 sc unworked: 8 sc.

Rows 2 and 3: Ch 1, turn; 2 sc in first sc, sc in next sc and in each sc across to last 2 sc, 2 sc in last sc: 12 sc.

Rows 4-24: Ch 1, turn; sc in each sc across.

Rows 25-27: Ch 1, turn; work beginning decrease, sc in next sc and in each sc across to last 2 sc, work ending decrease; finish off: 6 sc.

FRONT LEGS

Row 1: Ch 14, with **wrong** side of Belly facing, work beginning decrease; sc in next 2 sc, work ending decrease, ch 15: 4 sc and 29 chs.

Row 2: Turn; sc in back ridge of second ch from hook and in next 13 chs, 2 sc in next sc, sc in next 2 sc, 2 sc in next sc, sc in back ridge of last 14 chs: 34 sc.

Rows 3-6: Ch 1, turn; sc in each sc across.

Row 7: Ch 1, turn; sc in first 14 sc, 2 sc in next sc, sc in each sc across to last 15 sc, 2 sc in next sc, sc in last 14 sc: 36 sc.

Row 8: Ch 1, turn; sc in each sc across.

Rows 9-14: Repeat Rows 7 and 8, 3 times; do **not** finish off: 42 sc.

FRONT OF THIRD LEG

Row 1: Ch 1, turn; sc in first 8 sc, decrease, leave remaining 32 sc unworked: 9 sc.

Row 2: Ch 1, turn; work beginning decrease, sc in last 7 sc: 8 sc.

Row 3: Ch 1, turn; sc in first 6 sc, work ending decrease; finish off: 7 sc.

FRONT OF LAST LEG

Row 1: With **wrong** side of Front Legs facing, skip next 22 unworked sc and work joining decrease in next 2 sc; sc in last 8 sc: 9 sc.

Row 2: Ch 1, turn; sc in first 7 sc, work ending decrease: 8 sc.

Row 3: Ch 1, turn; work beginning decrease, sc in last 6 sc; finish off: 7 sc.

CHEST

Row 1: With **wrong** side of Front Legs facing and working in 22 unworked sc, skip first 8 sc and join yarn with sc in next sc; sc in same st and in next 4 sc, 2 sc in next sc, leave remaining 8 sc unworked: 8 sc.

Row 2: Ch 1, turn; sc in each sc across.

Row 3: Ch 1, turn; 2 sc in first sc, sc in next sc and in each sc across to last sc, 2 sc in last sc: 10 sc.

Row 4: Ch 1, turn; sc in each sc across.

Row 5: Ch 1, turn; 2 sc in first sc, sc in next sc and in each sc across to last sc, 2 sc in last sc: 12 sc.

Rows 6-31: Ch 1, turn; sc in each sc across.

Row 32: Ch 1, turn; sc in first 5 sc, decrease, sc in last 5 sc: 11 sc.

Rows 33-35: Ch 1, turn; work beginning decrease, sc in next sc and in each sc across to last 2 sc, work ending decrease: 5 sc.

Row 36: Ch 1, turn; sc in each sc across, finish off.

FINISHING

Matching stitches and ends of rows throughout:

Step 1: Working from **top** to **bottom** of Tail, sew long opening closed.

Step 2: Holding **wrong** sides of Top and Underneath of Body together, sew from where 4 unworked stitches at base of Tail and beginning of Bottom meet. Sew from two side stitches of Tail out to Back of Legs to close.

Step 3: Sew from Front of Back Legs, across Belly (side seams), and down Backs of Front Legs, making sure to leave openings for Soles of Back Feet.

Step 4: Sew Soles of Back Feet to bottom of each Back Leg.

Step 5: Begin adding fiberfill and continue to add as you work.

Step 6: Sew from Front of Front Legs across to center of where five stitches of muzzle and mouth meet.

Step 7: Sew Soles of Feet to bottom of each Front Leg.

Step 8: Using photo as a guide and long end, sew each Ear to Head.

Step 9: Stack Black button on top of White button to form eye. Using Black yarn, tie layered button eye in place. Repeat for second eye.

TOY SCOTTIE DOG SWEATER

Shown on page 65.

MATERIALS

Sport Weight Yarn:
Red ~ 5¹/₂ ounces, 560 yards
(160 grams, 512 meters)
White ~ 20 yards (18.5 meters)
Crochet hooks, size G (4 mm) **or**
size needed for gauge
Tapestry needle

GAUGE: 20 sc and 24 rows = 4" (10 cm)

Gauge Swatch: 4" (10 cm) square
With Red, ch 21.
Row 1: Sc in second ch from hook and in
each ch across: 20 sc.
Rows 2-24: Ch 1, turn; sc in each sc
across.
Finish off.

STITCH GUIDE

POPCORN
3 Sc in sc indicated changing to Red
in last sc made (**Fig. 5, page 94**),
drop loop from hook, insert hook in
first sc of 3-sc group, hook dropped
loop and draw through st.

SC DECREASE (uses next 2 sts)
Pull up a loop in next 2 sts, YO and
draw through all 3 loops on hook
(**counts as one sc**).

2-DC DECREASE (uses next 2 sts)
★ YO, insert hook in **next** st, YO and
pull up a loop, YO and draw through
2 loops on hook; repeat from ★ once
more, YO and draw through all
3 loops on hook (**counts as one dc**).

3-DC DECREASE (uses next 3 sts)
★ YO, insert hook in **next** st, YO and
pull up a loop, YO and draw through
2 loops on hook; repeat from ★ 2 times
more, YO and draw through all
4 loops on hook (**counts as one dc**).

SLEEVE (Make 2)
RIBBING
With Red, ch 16.

Row 1: Sc in back ridge of second ch
from hook (**Fig. 1, page 93**) and in each
ch across: 15 sc.

Row 2: Ch 1, turn; sc in Back Loop Only
of each sc across (**Fig. 2, page 93**).

Repeat Row 2 until 24 ribs (48 rows) are
complete.

Joining Row: Ch 1, turn; working in free
loops of beginning ch (**Fig. 3b, page 93**)
and in Back Loops Only of sc on last row,
slip st in each st across; do **not** finish off.

BODY
Rnd 1 (Right side): Ch 1, turn; matching
ends of rows, fold Ribbing in half with
wrong side together, working through
both thicknesses, sc in end of each row
around; join with slip st to first sc: 48 sc.

Note: Loop a short piece of yarn around
any stitch to mark Rnd 1 as **right** side.

Rnd 2: Ch 1, turn; sc in each sc around;
join with slip st to first sc.

Rnd 3: Ch 1, turn; working over White, with Red sc in first 15 sc changing to White in last sc made (**Fig. 5, *page* 94**), work Popcorn in next sc, ★ sc in next 15 sc changing to White in last sc made, work Popcorn in next sc; repeat from ★ once **more**; cut White; join with slip st to first sc: 45 sc and 3 Popcorns.

Continue changing colors in same manner throughout.

Rnd 4: Ch 1, turn; sc in each sc around; join with slip st to first sc.

Rnd 5: Ch 1, turn; sc in each sc around; join with slip st to first sc, finish off.

BODY
BOTTOM RIBBING
With Red, ch 16.

Row 1: Sc in back ridge of second ch from hook and in each ch across: 15 sc.

Row 2: Ch 1, turn; sc in Back Loop Only of each sc across.

Repeat Row 2 until 42 ribs (84 rows) are complete; do **not** finish off.

BODY
Row 1 (Right side): Ch 1, do **not** turn; matching end of rows, fold Ribbing in half with **wrong** side together, working through **both** thicknesses, 2 sc in end of first row, sc in end of each row across: 85 sc.

Note: Mark Row 1 as **right** side.

Rows 2-4: Ch 1, turn; sc in each sc across.

Row 5: Ch 1, turn; working over White, with Red sc in first 18 sc, with White work Popcorn in next sc, ★ with Red sc in next 15 sc, with White work Popcorn in next sc; repeat from ★ 2 times **more**, working over White, with Red sc in each sc across; cut White: 81 sc and 4 Popcorns.

Rows 6-16: Ch 1, turn; sc in each st across: 85 sc.

Row 17: Ch 1, turn; working over White, with Red sc in first 10 sc, with White work Popcorn in next sc, ★ with Red sc in next 15 sc, with White work Popcorn in next sc; repeat from ★ 3 times **more**, working over White, with Red sc in each sc across; cut White: 80 sc and 5 Popcorns.

Rows 18-21: Ch 1, turn; sc in each st across: 85 sc.

Row 22 (Joining rnd): Ch 1, turn; sc in first 3 sc, with **right** sides of one Sleeve and Body together, sc in next 16 sc, leave remaining 32 sc on Sleeve unworked; working on Body only, sc decrease, sc in next 43 sc; sc decrease, with **right** sides of remaining Sleeve and Body together, sc in next 16 sc, leave remaining 32 sc on Sleeve unworked; working on Body only, sc in last 3 sc: 83 sc.

Row 23: Ch 1, turn; sc in first 3 sc, working in unworked sc on Sleeve, sc decrease, sc in next 28 sc, sc decrease, working in sts on Body, sc decrease, sc in next 41 sc, sc decrease, working in unworked sc on Sleeve, sc decrease, sc in next 28 sc, sc decrease, working in sts on Body, sc in last 3 sc: 109 sc.

Continued on page 82.

Row 24: Ch 2, turn; skip first sc, dc in next sc, 2-dc decrease, sc in next 25 sc, hdc in next sc, dc in next sc, 2-dc decrease twice, dc in next sc, hdc in next sc, sc in next 35 sc, hdc in next sc, dc in next sc, 2-dc decrease twice, dc in next sc, hdc in next sc, sc in next 25 sc, 2-dc decrease twice: 101 sts.

Row 25: Ch 2, turn; 2-dc decrease, skip next 2 sc, sc in next 21 sc, hdc in next sc, dc in next hdc, 2-dc decrease twice, dc in next hdc, hdc in next sc, sc in next 33 sc, hdc in next sc, dc in next hdc, 2-dc decrease twice, dc in next hdc, hdc in next sc, sc in next 21 sc, skip next 2 sc, 3-dc decrease: 89 sts.

Row 26: Ch 3 **(counts as first dc, now and throughout)**, turn; skip next 2 sc, sc in next 18 sc, hdc in next sc, dc in next hdc, 2-dc decrease twice, dc in next hdc, hdc in next sc, sc in next 31 sc, hdc in next sc, dc in next hdc, 2-dc decrease twice, dc in next hdc, hdc in next sc, sc in next 18 sc, skip next 2 sc, dc in last dc: 81 sts.

Row 27: Ch 3, turn; skip next 2 sc, sc in next 15 sc, hdc in next sc, dc in next hdc, 2-dc decrease twice, dc in next hdc, hdc in next sc, sc in next 29 sc, hdc in next sc, dc in next hdc, 2-dc decrease twice, dc in next hdc, hdc in next sc, sc in next 15 sc, skip next 2 sc, dc in last dc; do **not** finish off: 73 sts.

NECK RIBBING

Foundation Row: Ch 3, turn; skip next 2 sc, sc in each sc across to last 3 sts, skip next 2 sc, dc in last dc: 69 sts.

Ch 16.

Row 1: Sc in back ridge of second ch from hook and in each ch across, slip st in first 2 sc on Foundation Row: 17 sts.

Row 2: Turn; skip first 2 slip sts, sc in Back Loop Only of each sc across: 15 sc.

Row 3: Ch 1, turn; sc in Back Loop Only of next 15 sc, slip st in **both** loops of next 2 sc on Foundation Row: 17 sts.

Repeat Rows 2 and 3 across, ending by working Row 2.

Last Row: Ch 1, turn; sc in Back Loop Only of next 15 sc, slip st in **both** loops of last sc on Foundation Row; finish off leaving a long end for sewing.

Fold Neck Ribbing in half with **wrong** side together. Sew in place along Foundation Row with long end.

EDGING
RIGHT SIDE

With **right** side facing and working through **both** thicknesses of Bottom Ribbing, join Red with sc in first sc (**see Joining With Sc, page 92**); sc evenly across, working through **both** thicknesses of Neck Ribbing; finish off.

LEFT SIDE

With **right** side facing and working through **both** thicknesses of Neck Ribbing, join Red with sc in first sc; sc evenly across working through **both** thicknesses of Bottom Ribbing; finish off.

Put Sweater on Scottie Dog; sew seam closed.

PURSES

Shown on page 83.

MATERIALS

Sport Weight Yarn:

Clutch Bag

- Black - 1¹/₂ ounces, 155 yards
  (40 grams, 141.5 meters)
- White - 20 yards (18.5 meters)
- Red - 10 yards (9 meters)
- Brown - 10 yards (9 meters)
- Green - 10 yards (9 meters)

Drawstring Purse

- Black - 3¹/₂ ounces, 355 yards
  (100 grams, 324.5 meters)
- White - 25 yards (23 meters)
- Green - 20 yards (18.5 meters)
- Red - 10 yards (9 meters)

Crochet hook, size F (3.75 mm) **or** size needed for gauge

6¹/₂" (16.5 cm) Plastic circle
(Drawstring Purse only)

Snap (Clutch Bag only)

Sewing needle and thread

Tapestry needle

STITCH GUIDE

POPCORN (uses one sc)
3 Sc in sc indicated changing to Black in last sc made (**Fig. 5**, *page 94*), drop loop from hook, insert hook in first sc of 3-sc group, hook dropped loop and draw through st.

BEGINNING DECREASE
Pull up a loop in same st and in next sc, YO and draw through all 3 loops on hook (**counts as one sc**).

DECREASE
Pull up a loop in next 2 sc, YO and draw through all 3 loops on hook (**counts as one sc**).

ENDING DECREASE
Pull up a loop in last 2 sc, YO and draw through all 3 loops on hook (**counts as one sc**).

CLUTCH BAG

Finished Size: 4"h x 8¹/₂"w
(10 cm x 21.5 cm)

GAUGE: 10 sc and 12 rows = 2" (5 cm)

Gauge Swatch: 2" (5 cm)
With Black, ch 11.
Row 1: Sc in second ch from hook and in each ch across: 10 sc.
Rows 2-12: Ch 1, turn; sc in each sc across.
Finish off.

BODY

With Black, ch 46.

Row 1 (Right side)**:** Sc in back ridge of second ch from hook (**Fig. 1**, *page 93*) and each ch across: 45 sc.

Note: Loop a short piece of yarn around any sc to mark Row 1 as **right** side.

Row 2: Ch 1, turn; sc in each sc across.

Row 3: Ch 1, turn; working over White with Black, sc in first 2 sc changing to White in last sc made (**Fig. 5**, *page 94*), work Popcorn in next sc, ★ working over White, sc in next 7 sc changing to White in last sc made, work Popcorn in next sc; repeat from ★ across to last 2 sc, working over White, sc in last 2 sc, cut White.

Continue to change colors in same manner.

Rows 4-8: Ch 1, turn; sc in each st across.

Row 9: Ch 1, turn; working over White, with Black sc in first 6 sc, with White work Popcorn in next sc, ★ with Black sc in next 7 sc, with White work Popcorn in next sc; repeat from ★ across to last 6 sc, working over White, with Black sc in last 6 sc; cut White.

Rows 10-14: Ch 1, turn; sc in same st and in each sc across.

Rows 15-68: Repeat Rows 3-14, 4 times; then repeat Rows 3-8 once **more**.

Joining: Fold Body with **right** side together and matching beginning ch to top of Row 50; with front facing and working in ends of rows through **both** thicknesses, join Black with slip st at fold, slip st in next 24 rows; working around flap, sc in next 18 rows; working in sc across Row 68, 3 sc in first sc, sc in next sc and in each sc across to last sc, 3 sc in last sc; working in ends of rows, sc in next 18 rows; working in ends of rows through **both** thicknesses, slip st in next 25 rows; finish off.

Turn Bag **right** side out.

CHERRY (Make 2)
Rnd 1 (Right side): With Red, ch 2, 6 sc in second ch from hook; do **not** join, place marker (**see Markers, page 93**).

Rnd 2: 2 Sc in each sc around: 12 sc.

Rnds 3-5: Sc in each sc around.

Stuff firmly with Red yarn.

Rnds 6 and 7: Decrease around: 3 sc.

Finish off.

STEM
Join Brown with slip st at top of one Cherry; ch 1, turn; sc in slip st, **turn**; sc in horizontal loop at left side of sc (**Fig. 1a, page 36**), ★ **turn**; sc in horizontal loops at left side of sc (**Fig. 1b, page 36**); repeat from ★ until Stem measures 3"; finish off.

Repeat for second Cherry until Stem measures 2¹/₂".

LEAF (Make 2)
Foundation Row: Ch 2, sc in second ch from hook: one sc.

Rnd 1 (Right side): Ch 1, turn; 3 sc in Front Loop Only of sc (**Fig. 2, page 93**), **turn**; 3 sc in free loop of same sc (**Fig. 3a, page 93**); join with slip st to **both** loops of first sc: 6 sc.

Rnd 2: Ch 1, do **not** turn; working in both loops, 2 sc in first sc, sc in next sc, 2 sc in each of next 2 sc, sc in next sc, 2 sc in last sc; join with slip st to first sc: 10 sc.

Rnds 3-5: Ch 1, sc in each sc around; join with slip st to first sc.

Rnd 6: Ch 1, work beginning decrease, sc in next sc, decrease twice, sc in next sc, work ending decrease; join with slip st to first sc: 6 sc.

Rnd 7: Ch 1, pull up a loop in first 3 sc, YO and draw through all 4 loops on hook, pull up a loop in last 3 sc, YO and draw through all 4 loops on hook; join with slip st to first st, finish off.

Using photo as a guide for placement:

Sew Stems together, then sew Leaves to Stems.

Sew Cherries to flap of Purse.

Sew on snap.

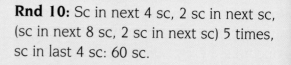

DRAWSTRING PURSE
Finished Size: 7½" (19 cm) tall

GAUGE: Rnds 1-4 = 2" (5 cm)
10 sc and 12 rows = 2" (5 cm)

Gauge Swatch: 2" (5 cm)
Work same as Center for 4 rnds.
Finish off.

BOTTOM
FIRST HALF
Rnd 1 (Right side): With Black, ch 2, 6 sc in second ch from hook; do **not** join, place marker **(see Markers, page 90)**.

Note: Loop a short piece of yarn around any sc to mark Rnd 1 as **right** side.

Rnd 2: 2 Sc in each sc around: 12 sc.

Rnd 3: (Sc in next sc, 2 sc in next sc) around: 18 sc.

Rnd 4: (2 Sc in next sc, sc in next 2 sc) around: 24 sc.

Rnd 5: (Sc in next 3 sc, 2 sc in next sc) around: 30 sc.

Rnd 6: (2 Sc in next sc, sc in next 4 sc) around: 36 sc.

Rnd 7: (Sc in next 5 sc, 2 sc in next sc) around: 42 sc.

Rnd 8: (2 Sc in next sc, sc in next 6 sc) around: 48 sc.

Rnd 9: (Sc in next 7 sc, 2 sc in next sc) around: 54 sc.

Rnd 10: Sc in next 4 sc, 2 sc in next sc, (sc in next 8 sc, 2 sc in next sc) 5 times, sc in last 4 sc: 60 sc.

Rnd 11: (Sc in next 9 sc, 2 sc in next sc) around: 66 sc.

Rnd 12: (2 Sc in next sc, sc in next 10 sc) around: 72 sc.

Rnd 13: Sc in next 5 sc, 2 sc in next sc, (sc in next 11 sc, 2 sc in next sc) 5 times, sc in last 6 sc: 78 sc.

Rnd 14: (Sc in next 12 sc, 2 sc in next sc) around: 84 dc.

Rnd 15: (2 Sc in next sc, sc in next 13 sc) around: 90 sc.

Rnd 16: Sc in next 7 sc, 2 sc in next sc, (sc in next 14 sc, 2 sc in next sc) 5 times, sc in next 7 sc: 96 sc.

Rnd 17: (Sc in next 15 sc, 2 sc in next sc) around: 102 sc.

Rnd 18: (2 Sc in next sc, sc in next 16 sc) around; slip st in first sc, finish off: 108 sc.

SECOND HALF
Work same as First Half; do **not** finish off: 108 sc.

JOINING
Ch 1, with **wrong** sides of Bottom Halves together and Second Half facing, 2 sc in same st, sc in next 26 sc, (2 sc in next sc, sc in next 26 sc) around inserting plastic circle before closing; join with slip st to first sc, do **not** finish off: 112 sc.

SIDES

Rnds 1-3: Ch 1, **turn**; sc in same st and in each sc around; join with slip st to first sc.

Rnd 4: Ch 1, turn; working over White, with Black sc in same st and in next 6 sc changing to White in last sc made **(Fig. 5, page 94)**, work Popcorn in next sc, ★ working over White, sc in next 7 sc changing to White in last sc made, work Popcorn in next sc; repeat from ★ around, cut White; join with slip st to first sc.

Continue to change colors in same manner.

Rnds 5-9: Ch 1, turn; sc in same st and in each sc around; join with slip st to first sc.

Rnd 10: Ch 1, turn; working over White, with Black sc in same st and in next 3 sc, with White work Popcorn in next sc, ★ with Black sc in next 7 sc, with White work Popcorn in next sc; repeat from ★ around to last 3 sc, working over White, with Black sc in last 3 sc; join with slip st to first sc, cut White.

Rnds 11-15: Ch 1, turn; sc in same st and in each sc around; join with slip st to first sc.

Rnds 16-33: Repeat Rnds 4-15 once, then repeat Rnds 4-9 once **more**.

Rnd 34 (Eyelet rnd): Ch 4 **(counts as first dc plus ch 1)**, turn; skip next sc, (dc in next sc, ch 1, skip next sc) around; join with slip st to first dc: 56 ch-1 sps.

Rnd 35: Ch 1, turn; sc in same st and in each ch-1 sp and each dc around; join with slip st to first sc: 112 sc.

Rnds 36-39: Ch 1, turn; sc in same st and in each sc around; join with slip st to first sc.

Rnds 40-45: Repeat Rnds 10-15.

Finish off.

CHERRY (Make 2)

Work same as Clutch Bag Cherry, page 85.

DRAWSTRING (Make 2)

With Green, ch 2, sc in second ch from hook, turn; sc in horizontal loop at left side of sc **(Fig. 1a, page 36)**, ★ turn; sc in horizontal loops at left side of sc **(Fig. 1b, page 36)**; repeat from ★ until Drawstring measures 24"; finish off.

Weave one Drawstring through ch-1 sps on Eyelet Rnd, sew ends together. Beginning on opposite side as first Drawstring, weave second Drawstring through same ch-1 sps on Eyelet Rnd, sew ends together.

Attach one Cherry to each Drawstring.

PINCUSHION
Shown on page 83.

MATERIALS
Bedspread Weight Cotton Thread (size 10):
- Yellow - 115 yards (105 meters)
- Red - 13 yards (12 meters)
- White - 11 yards (10 meters)
- Black - 10 yards (9 meters)
- Pink - 5 yards (4.5 meters)
- Blue - 5 yards (4.5 meters)
- Green - 3 yards (2.5 meters)

Steel crochet hook, size 7 (1.65 mm) **or** size needed for gauge
Tapestry needle
Polyester fiberfill
2⅝" (6.75 cm) Plastic circle

GAUGE SWATCH: 2⅝" (6.75 cm) diameter
Work same as Body through Rnd 6.

STITCH GUIDE

BACK POST SINGLE CROCHET (*abbreviated* BP*sc*)
Insert hook from **back** to **front** around post of dc indicated (**Fig. 4, page** 93), YO and pull up a loop, YO and draw through both loops on hook. Skip dc in front of BPsc.

BEGINNING SC DECREASE (uses first 2 sts)
Pull up a loop in first 2 sts, YO and draw through all 3 loops on hook (**counts as one sc**).

SC DECREASE (uses next 2 sts)
Pull up a loop in next 2 sts, YO and draw through all 3 loops on hook (**counts as one sc**).

DC DECREASE (uses next 2 sts)
★ YO, insert hook in **next** st, YO and pull up a loop, YO and draw through 2 loops on hook; repeat from ★ once **more**, YO and draw through all 3 loops on hook (**counts as one dc**).

3-HDC CLUSTER (uses next 3 sts)
★ YO, insert hook in **next** st, YO and pull up a loop; repeat from ★ 2 times **more**, YO and draw through all 7 loops on hook.

3-DC CLUSTER (uses next 3 dc)
★ YO, insert hook in **next** dc, YO and pull up a loop, YO and draw through 2 loops on hook; repeat from ★ 2 times **more**, YO and draw through all 4 loops on hook.

BODY

Rnd 1 (Right side): With Yellow, ch 4, 11 dc in fourth ch from hook; join with slip st to top of beginning ch: 12 sts.

Note: Loop a short piece of thread around any stitch to mark Rnd 1 as **right** side.

Rnd 2: Ch 3 (**counts as first dc, now and throughout**), dc in same st, 2 dc in next dc and in each dc around; join with slip st to first dc: 24 dc.

Rnd 3: Ch 3, 2 dc in next dc, (dc in next dc, 2 dc in next dc) around; join with slip st to first dc: 36 dc.

Rnd 4: Ch 3, dc in next dc, 2 dc in next dc, (dc in next 2 dc, 2 dc in next dc) around; join with slip st to first dc: 48 dc.

Rnd 5: Ch 3, 2 dc in next dc, (dc in next dc, 2 dc in next dc) around; join with slip st to first dc: 72 dc.

Rnd 6: Ch 3, dc in next dc, 2 dc in next dc, (dc in next 2 dc, 2 dc in next dc) around; join with slip st to first dc: 96 dc.

Rnd 7: Ch 1, work BPsc around same st and each dc around; join with slip st to first BPsc.

Rnds 8-11: Ch 3, dc in next st and in each st around; join with slip st to first dc.

Rnd 12: Ch 3, dc in next 6 dc, 2 dc in next dc, (dc in next 7 dc, 2 dc in next dc) around; join with slip st to first dc: 108 dc.

Rnds 13-16: Ch 3, dc in next dc and in each dc around; join with slip st to first dc.

Rnd 17: Ch 3, dc in next 6 dc, dc decrease, (dc in next 7 dc, dc decrease) around; join with slip st to first dc: 96 dc.

Rnd 18: Ch 3, dc in next dc and in each dc around; join with slip st to first dc.

Rnd 19: Ch 3, dc in next 5 dc, dc decrease, (dc in next 6 dc, dc decrease) around; join with slip st to first dc: 84 dc.

Rnd 20: Ch 3, dc in next 4 dc, dc decrease, (dc in next 5 dc, dc decrease) around; join with slip st to first dc: 72 dc.

Rnd 21: Ch 3, dc in next 3 dc, dc decrease, (dc in next 4 dc, dc decrease) around; join with slip st to first dc: 60 dc.

Rnd 22: Ch 1, work BPsc around same st and each dc around; join with slip st to first BPsc.

Rnd 23: Ch 3, dc in next BPsc and in each BPsc around; join with slip st to first dc.

Rnd 24: Ch 3, dc in next 2 dc, dc decrease, (dc in next 3 dc, dc decrease) around; join with slip st to first dc: 48 dc.

Rnd 25: Ch 3, dc in next dc, dc decrease, (dc in next 2 dc, dc decrease) around; join with slip st to first dc: 36 dc.

Rnd 26: Ch 2, dc in next dc, dc decrease around; skip beginning ch-2 and join with slip st to first dc: 18 dc.

Inserting plastic circle first, stuff Body with polyester fiberfill.

Rnd 27: Ch 2, dc decrease, work 3-dc Cluster around; skip beginning ch-2 and join with slip st to first dc; finish off leaving a long end for sewing.

RIM

Rnd 1: With Rnd 27 facing and working in skipped dc on Rnd 21, join Black with slip st in first dc; ch 3, 2 dc in next dc, dc in next dc changing to White (**Fig. 5, page 94**), dc in next dc, 2 dc in next dc, dc in next dc changing to Black, ★ dc in next dc, 2 dc in next dc, dc in next dc changing to White, dc in next dc, 2 dc in next dc, dc in next dc changing to Black; repeat from ★ around; join with slip st to first dc: 80 dc.

Continue to change colors in same manner throughout.

Rnd 2: Ch 3, dc in next 3 dc, with White dc in next 4 dc, ★ with Black dc in next 4 dc, with White dc in next 4 dc; repeat from ★ around; join with slip st to first dc, finish off both colors.

Continued on page 90.

SPOUT

With Yellow and leaving a long end for sewing, ch 23; being careful not to twist ch, join with slip st to form a ring.

Rnd 1 (Right side): Ch 1, sc in same st and in next 5 chs, hdc in next 3 chs, dc in next 5 chs, hdc in next 3 chs, sc in last 6 chs; join with slip st to first sc: 23 sts.

Note: Mark Rnd 1 as **right** side.

Rnd 2: Ch 1, sc in first 8 sts, hdc in next 2 sts, dc in next 3 dc, hdc in next 2 sts, sc in last 8 sts; join with slip st to first sc.

Rnd 3: Ch 1, sc in first 8 sc, hdc in next 2 hdc, dc in next dc, 2 dc in next dc, dc in next dc, hdc in next 2 hdc, sc in last 8 sc; join with slip st to first sc: 24 sts.

Rnd 4: Ch 1, sc in first 6 sc, hdc in next 2 sc, dc in next 3 sts, 2 dc in each of next 2 dc, dc in next 3 sts, hdc in next 2 sc, sc in last 6 sc; join with slip st to first sc: 26 sts.

Rnd 5: Ch 1, sc in first sc, (sc decrease, sc in next st) twice, hdc in next 2 sts, dc in next 8 dc, hdc in next 2 sts, sc in next hdc, (sc decrease, sc in next sc) twice; join with slip st to first sc: 22 sts.

Rnd 6: Ch 2, hdc in next 6 sts, dc in next 8 dc, hdc in last 7 sts; join with slip st to top of beginning ch-2.

Rnd 7: Ch 2, hdc in next 4 hdc, dc in next 12 sts, hdc in last 5 hdc; join with slip st to top of beginning ch-2.

Rnd 8: Ch 3, dc in next st and in each st around; join with slip st to first dc.

Rnd 9: Ch 3, (dc decrease, dc in next dc) around; join with slip st to first dc: 15 dc.

Rnd 10: Ch 2, working in Back Loops Only (**Fig. 2,** *page* 93), (YO, insert hook in **next** dc, YO and pull up a loop) twice, YO and draw through all 5 loops on hook (**beginning Cluster**), work 3-hdc Clusters around; join with slip st to top of beginning Cluster, finish off.

Rnd 11: With **right** side facing and working in free loops of dc on Rnd 9 (**Fig. 3a,** *page 93*), join Yellow with slip st in first dc; ch 2, hdc in same st and in next 3 dc, dc in next 3 dc, 3 dc in next dc, dc in next 3 dc, hdc in next 3 dc, 2 hdc in last dc; join with slip st to top of beginning ch-2, finish off.

HANDLE

With White and leaving a long end for sewing, ch 14.

Row 1 (Right side): Dc in fourth ch from hook (**3 skipped chs count as first dc**) and in each ch across: 12 dc.

Row 2: Ch 3, turn; dc in next dc and in each dc across changing to Black in last dc made; do **not** cut White.

Row 3: Ch 3, turn; dc in next dc and in each dc across.

Row 4: Ch 3, turn; dc in next dc and in each dc across changing to White in last dc made; do **not** cut Black.

Carry unused thread **loosely** along edge.

Row 5: Ch 2 (**counts as first hdc, now and throughout**), turn; hdc in next 2 dc, dc in next 6 dc, hdc in last 3 dc.

Row 6: Ch 2, turn; hdc in next 2 hdc, dc in next 6 dc, hdc in last 3 hdc changing to Black in last hdc made.

Row 7: Ch 2, turn; hdc in next 2 hdc, dc in next 6 dc, hdc in last 3 hdc.

Row 8: Ch 2, turn; hdc in next 2 hdc, dc in next 6 dc, hdc in last 3 hdc changing to White in last hdc made.

Row 9: Ch 2, turn; hdc in next 2 hdc, dc in next 6 dc, hdc in last 3 hdc.

Rows 10-17: Repeat Rows 6-9 twice.

Row 18: Ch 2, turn; hdc in next 2 hdc, dc in next 6 dc, hdc in last 3 hdc; finish off both colors leaving long ends for sewing.

Fold Handle along long edge with **right** side facing. Using corresponding colors and matching rows, sew long edge together. Stuff with polyester fiberfill.

LARGE FLOWER
BODY
Rnd 1 (Wrong side): With Yellow and leaving a long end for sewing, ch 3, 6 hdc in third ch from hook; skip beginning ch and join with slip st to first hdc: 6 hdc.

Rnd 2: Working **around** Rnd 1, work 10 sc in same ch as previous rnd; join with slip st to first sc, finish off.

Rnd 3: With **right** side facing, join Red with slip st in any sc; ch 3, dc in same st, 2 dc in next sc and in each sc around; join with slip st to first dc, finish off leaving a long end for sewing.

LEAF (Make 2)
Foundation Row: With Green, ch 6, sc in second ch from hook and in each ch across: 5 sc.

Rnd 1: Ch 1, turn; working in Front Loops Only, sc in each sc across, **turn**; working in free loops of same sc, sc in each sc across; join with slip st to **both** loops of first sc: 10 sc.

Rnd 2: Ch 1, do **not** turn; working in both loops, sc in each sc around; join with slip st to first sc.

Rnd 3: Ch 1, work beginning sc decrease, sc in next sc, sc decrease twice, sc in next sc, sc decrease; join with slip st to first sc: 6 sc.

Rnd 4: Ch 1, work beginning sc decrease, sc decrease twice; join with slip st to first sc, finish off.

SMALL FLOWER (Make 12)
Rnd 1 (Right side): With Yellow, ch 2, 6 sc in second ch from hook; join with slip st to first sc, finish off.

Rnd 2: With **wrong** side facing, join Blue, Pink or Red with slip st in any sc; ch 2, hdc in same st, 2 hdc in each sc around; join with slip st to first hdc, finish off leaving a long end for sewing.

FINISHING
Using photo as a guide for placement:

Fold Rim with **wrong** side together. With Yellow, tack Rnd 2 of Rim to Rnd 21 of Body.

Sew Handle to Teapot along Row 8 and Row 18 of Handle under Rim edge.

Sew Spout to Teapot opposite Handle, stuffing with polyester fiberfill before closing.

Sew Large Flower and Leaves to top of Teapot, stuffing Large Flower firmly before closing.

Sew Small Flowers to top along Rim edge.

GENERAL INSTRUCTIONS

ABBREVIATIONS

BPsc	Back Post single crochet(s)
ch(s)	chain(s)
cm	centimeters
dc	double crochet(s)
dtr	double treble crochet(s)
FPsc	Front Post single crochet(s)
hdc	half double crochet(s)
mm	millimeters
Rnd(s)	Round(s)
sc	single crochet(s)
sp(s)	space(s)
st(s)	stitch(es)
tr	treble crochet(s)
YO	yarn over

★ — work instructions following ★ as many **more** times as indicated in addition to the first time.

† to † — work all instructions from first † to second † **as many** times as specified.

( ) or [ ] — work enclosed instructions **as many** times as specified by the number immediately following **or** work all enclosed instructions in the stitch or space indicated **or** contains explanatory remarks.

colon (:) — the number(s) given after a colon at the end of a row or round denote(s) the number of stitches or spaces you should have on that row or round.

GAUGE

Exact gauge is **essential** for proper size or fit. Before beginning your project, make the sample swatch given in the individual instructions in the yarn or thread and hook specified. After completing the swatch, measure it, counting your stitches and rows or rounds carefully. If your swatch is larger or smaller than specified, **make another, changing hook size to get the correct gauge**. Keep trying until you find the size hook that will give you the specified gauge. Once proper gauge is obtained, measure width of garment or afghan approximately every 3" (7.5 cm) to be sure gauge remains consistent.

JOINING WITH SC

When instructed to join with sc, begin with a slip knot on hook. Insert hook in stitch or space indicated, YO and pull up a loop, YO and draw through both loops on hook.

CROCHET TERMINOLOGY	
UNITED STATES	**INTERNATIONAL**
slip stitch (slip st)	= single crochet (sc)
single crochet (sc)	= double crochet (dc)
half double crochet (hdc)	= half treble crochet (htr)
double crochet (dc)	= treble crochet (tr)
treble crochet (tr)	= double treble crochet (dtr)
double treble crochet (dtr)	= triple treble crochet (ttr)
skip	= miss

ALUMINUM CROCHET HOOKS													
U.S.	B-1	C-2	D-3	E-4	F-5	G-6	H-8	I-9	J-10	K-10½	N	P	Q
Metric - mm	2.25	2.75	3.25	3.5	3.75	4	5	5.5	6	6.5	9	10	15

STEEL CROCHET HOOKS																
U.S.	00	0	1	2	3	4	5	6	7	8	9	10	11	12	13	14
Metric - mm	3.5	3.25	2.75	2.25	2.1	2	1.9	1.8	1.65	1.5	1.4	1.3	1.1	1	.85	.75

JOINING WITH HDC

When instructed to join with hdc, begin with a slip knot on hook. YO, holding loop on hook, insert hook in stitch or space indicated, YO and pull up a loop (3 loops on hook), YO and draw through all 3 loops on hook.

JOINING WITH DC

When instructed to join with dc, begin with a slip knot on hook. YO, holding loop on hook, insert hook in stitch or space indicated, YO and pull up a loop (3 loops on hook), (YO and draw through 2 loops on hook) twice.

JOINING WITH TR

When instructed to join with tr, begin with a slip knot on hook. YO twice, holding loops on hook, insert hook in stitch or space indicated, YO and pull up a loop (4 loops on hook), (YO and draw through 2 loops on hook) 3 times.

MARKERS

Markers are used to help distinguish the beginning of each round being worked. Place a 2" (5 cm) scrap piece of yarn or thread before the first stitch of each round, moving marker after each round is complete.

BACK RIDGE

Work only in loops indicated by arrows (**Fig. 1**).

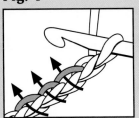

Fig. 1

BACK OR FRONT LOOP ONLY

Work only in loop(s) indicated by arrow (**Fig. 2**).

Fig. 2

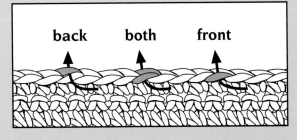

FREE LOOPS

After working in Back or Front Loops Only on a row or round, there will be a ridge of unused loops. These are called the free loops. Later, when instructed to work in the free loops of the same row or round, work in these loops (**Fig. 3a**).

When instructed to work in free loops of a chain, work in loop indicated by arrow (**Fig. 3b**).

Fig. 3a 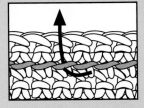   Fig. 3b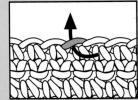

POST STITCH

Work around post of stitch indicated, inserting hook in direction of arrow (**Fig. 4**).

Fig. 4

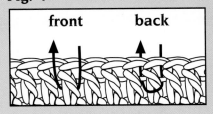

93

CHANGING COLORS

Work the last stitch to within one step of completion, hook new yarn (**Fig. 5**) and draw through all loops on hook. Cut old yarn and work over both ends if indicated or work **over** color not being used, holding it with normal tension.

Fig. 5

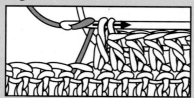

ADDING ON SINGLE CROCHETS

When instructed to add on sc at the end of a row, insert hook into base of last st (**Fig. 6**), YO and pull up a loop, YO and draw through one loop on hook, YO and draw through both loops on hook. Repeat as many times as instructed.

Fig. 6

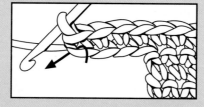

ADDING ON HALF DOUBLE CROCHETS

When instructed to add on hdc at the end of a row, YO, insert hook into base of last st (**Fig. 7**), YO and pull up a loop, YO and draw through one loop on hook, YO and draw through all 3 loops on hook. Repeat as many times as instructed.

Fig. 7

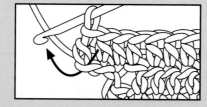

ADDING ON DOUBLE CROCHETS

When instructed to add on dc at the end of a row, YO, insert hook into base of last st (**Fig. 8**), YO and pull up a loop, YO and draw through one loop on hook, (YO and draw through 2 loops on hook) twice. Repeat as many times as instructed.

Fig. 8

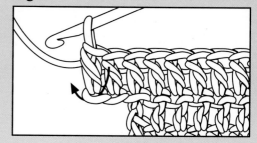

REVERSE SINGLE CROCHET

Working from **left** to **right**, ★ insert hook in st to right of hook (**Fig. 9a**), YO and draw through, under and to left of loop on hook (2 loops on hook) (**Fig. 9b**), YO and draw through both loops on hook (**Fig. 9c**) (**reverse sc made, Fig. 9d**); repeat from ★ around.

Fig. 9a

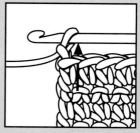

Fig. 9b

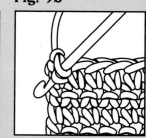

Fig. 9c

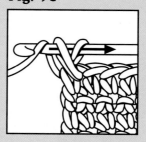

Fig. 9d

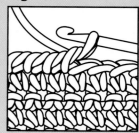

CROSS STITCH

Each square on the chart represents one full cross stitch and each triangle represents a quarter stitch. Each stitch is worked over one single crochet. Using a yarn needle and one strand of yarn, weave end of yarn under several stitches on back of Afghan or Pillow to secure (do not tie a knot). Work all stitches on **right** side of Afghan or Pillow. For horizontal rows, work stitches in two journeys by coming up at 1 and going down at 2. On the return journey, come up at 3 and go down at 4 **(Fig. 10)**. All stitches should be crossed in same direction. For vertical rows, complete each stitch individually.

A Quarter stitch is worked as follows: Come up at 1 and go down at 2 (in the middle of the single crochet).

Fig. 10

CHERRIES DIAGRAM

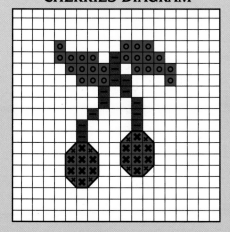

KEY

- ✖ - **RED**
- ▦ - **BROWN**
- ◉ - **GREEN**
- ◢ - **RED BACKSTITCH**

BACKSTITCH

For outlines and details, backstitch should be worked after the cross stitch design has been completed. Using one strand of yarn, come up at 1, go down at 2, then come up at 3 and go down at 4 **(Fig. 11)**.

Fig. 11

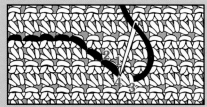

WASHING AND BLOCKING

For a more professional look, pieces should be washed and blocked. Using a mild detergent and warm water and being careful not to rub, twist, or wring, gently squeeze suds through the piece. Rinse several times in cool, clear water. Roll piece in a clean terry towel and gently press out the excess moisture. Lay piece on a flat surface and shape to proper size; where needed, pin in place using rust-proof pins. Allow to dry **completely**.

DIAGRAM

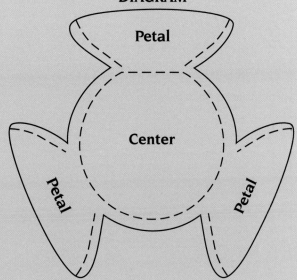

MATERIALS INFORMATION

Any brand of yarn or thread in the weights indicated in each project may be used to make these projects. It is best to refer to the yardage/meters when determining how many balls or skeins to purchase. Remember, to arrive at the finished size, it is the GAUGE/TENSION that is most important, not the brand of yarn or thread.

For your convenience, listed below are the specific yarns and threads used to create our photography models.

1. KITCHEN COMFORTS
Hot Pads, Placemat,
Tea Pot Cozy, and Napkin Ring
Bernat® Handicrafter® 100% Cotton
Worsted Weight Yarn:
 Red - #16 Red
 Green - #17 Emerald
 White - #01 White
 Black - #44 Black
 Yellow - #89 Banana Yellow
 Brown - #13130 Warm Brown

Scottie Dog for Napkin Ring only
Lily® Sugar'n Cream® 100% Cotton
Sport Weight Yarn
 Black - #19 Black

Magnets and Edgings
South Maid® Bedspread Weight
Cotton Thread (size 10):
 Ecru - #429 New Ecru
 Red - #491 Christmas Red
 Green - #484 Myrtle Green
 Yellow - #421 Goldenrod
 Black - #12 Black
 Brown - #434 Cappuccino

Rugs
Lily® Sugar'n Cream® Crafter's Cotton™
Bulky Weight Yarn:
 Red - #113 Country Red
 Yellow - #103 Yellow
 Green - #112 Green
 Black - #114 Black
 White - #100 White

2. COZY DEN
Afghan and Pillows
Worsted Weight Yarn:
 Yellow - Bernat® Berella "4"®
  #8887 Pale Tapestry Gold
 Orange - Bernat® Berella "4"®
  #1605 Burnt Orange
 Green - Bernat® Christmas
  #92708 Christmas Green
 Red - Bernat® Berella "4"®
  #8929 Geranium
 Blue - Red Heart® Super Saver
  #885 Delft Blue

Rug
Lily® Sugar'n Cream® Crafter's Cotton™
Bulky Weight Yarn:
 Red - #113 Country Red
 Yellow - #103 Yellow
 Green - #112 Green

3. BEDROOM WHIMSIES
Worsted Weight Yarn:
 Aran - Bernat® Berella "4" ®#8940 Natural
 Black - Bernat® Berella "4" ®#8994 Black
 Brown - Bernat® Berella "4" ®
  #1011 Soft Taupe
 Green - Bernat® Christmas
  #92708 Christmas Green
 Red - Bernat® Berella "4" ®
  #8929 Geranium

4. FLUFF 'N' STUFF
Child's Pullover, Toy Scottie Dog Sweater,
and Purses
Patons® Astra Sport Weight Yarn:
 Red - #2762 Cardinal
 White - #2751 White
 Black - #2765 Black
 Green - #2939 Kelly Green
Red Heart® Sport Weight Yarn
 Brown - #322 Fawn Beige

Toy Scottie Dog
Red Heart® Super Saver
Worsted Weight Yarn:
 Black - #312 Black

Pincushion
South Maid® Bedspread Weight
Cotton Thread (size 10):
 Yellow - #143 Soft Yellow
 Black - #12 Black
 White - #1 White
 Red - #491 Christmas Red
 Green - #484 Myrtle Green

We have made every effort to ensure that these instructions are accurate and complete. We cannot, however, be responsible for human error, typographical mistakes, or variations in individual work.

Photo models made and instructions tested by Janet Akins, Marianna Crowder, Raymelle Greening, Dale Potter, Donna Soellner, Margaret Taverner, and Mary Valen.